NEWMAN'S OWN COOKBOOK

Compiled by
Ursula Hotchner and Nell Newman
with
Trenchant Observations
and Diversions by
A. E. Hotchner

Paul Newman and his longtime friend and cooking partner A. E. Hotchner, with the help of Joanne Woodward, daughter Nell, and Ursula Hotchner, are constantly testing, refining, and developing new recipes. Herein, you'll find fun, easy, delectable ideas for your own culinary creations that, until now, only friends and neighbors of the Newmans have had the opportunity to enjoy.

NEWMAN'S OWN COOKBOOK

Compiled by

URSULA HOTCHNER

NELL NEWMAN

A. E. HOTCHNER

John Curley & Associates, Inc.
South Yarmouth, Ma.

Library of Congress Cataloging in Publication Data

Newman, Paul, 1925–
    Newman's own cookbook.

    1. Cookery.   2. Large type books.   I. Hotchner, Ursula.
II. Newman, Nell.   III. Hotchner, A. E.   IV Title
[TX715.N567   1987]   641.5   87–8847
ISBN 1–55504–285–6

Color photos by Arthur Rothstein.
Black and white photos by S. D. Colhoun.
Food Consultant: Susan Chesnoff.

Published in Large Print by arrangement with Contemporary Books, Inc. in the United States, territories and Canada.

Printed in Great Britain

All the recipes in this book
have been tested by preparing them
and serving them
to people with fussy appetites,
who have consumed them with relish.

CONTENTS

PART III
THE UNTOLD TALE OF NEWMAN'S OWN
103

PREFACE

It's our belief that eating well is the best revenge, and the recipes collected herein have been chosen with that in mind. These are our favorite recipes, created by us and our families, plus some created by a few special friends.

In choosing the recipes, our guidelines were that the dishes be simple, all natural, and imaginative. So don't expect to find exotic game birds floating in a cream and brandy sauce or lobster stuffed with caviar and foie gras.

These are the kind of wholesome, tasty dishes that would bring joy to the hearts of Butch Cassidy and Ernest Hemingway if the two of them happened to have dinner together.

P. L. Newman and A. E. Hotchner

PART I

THE
CONTRIBUTORS

PAUL NEWMAN

Paul Newman's principal vocation is cooking, and his reputation rests primarily on his culinary creations, specifically his revolutionary salad dressing, his indescribable scrod, his exemplary hamburger, and a spaghetti sauce that is the envy of Italian mothers. In what little time he is not occupied in the kitchen, Paul has managed, as an avocation, to dabble in films. A few of these, notably *Butch Cassiday and the Sundance Kid, The Sting, The Hustler, Hud, Cool Hand Luke,* and *The Verdict,* have become almost as well known as the dishes he has created.

Newman has also carved a unique niche for himself in the racing world, for he is the only driver on the race circuit who has managed to combine cooking and driving. Before the big races, Paul invariably chefs a lavish spread for his racing crew, as the photos will attest. In fact, Newman attributes his fast track times to the meals he prepares and consumes before he gets behind the wheel. In 1982, when he won the U.S. championship at Atlanta, his pregame meal consisted of Tomato and Endive Salad, a Newmanburger (see pages 32 and 62 for recipes), and a bag of his special brand of popcorn.

A. E. HOTCHNER

A. E. Hotchner has written nine books and four plays, and in one way or another food has found its way into all of them. In *Papa Hemingway*, which was published in twenty-six languages in thirty-eight countries, there are vivid descriptions of memorable meals with Hemingway and dishes that Hemingway particularly liked. Of course, some of the dishes, like Hemingway's predilection for peanut butter on rye with a thick slice of Bermuda onion on top for breakfast, may not set you to licking your chops, but some of the other Hemingway-inspired dishes – e.g., the Hotch Potch (see page 56) – definitely will.

Hotch has graphically described meals in some of his novels, most recently in *The Man Who Lived at the Ritz*. In an earlier book, *King of the Hill*, Hotch depicted a summer of his life when he was twelve when there was no food on the table, and to assuage his hunger he sometimes cut food ads from magazines and ate them. His dishes in this book, which he has shared generously with the Newman family and friends, demonstrate how far up the gourmet ladder he had climbed.

Newman and Hotchner have been buddies since 1956 when Newman starred in *The Battler*, a play Hotchner had written for NBC. They have co-owned several fishing boats over the past twenty years but have never caught an edible fish. But they are not above stopping at the local fish store on the way home and pretending that the store-bought sea bass or sole which they cook for dinner was hooked on the end of their line after a desperate struggle.

NELL NEWMAN

It may well be that the dishes Nell Newman cooks for her family were originally motivated by a desire to increase her school allowance, but by now, although she is still in college, her love of kitchen puttering has overtaken all else.

She is not a meat person, so her cooking leans toward vegetarian dishes, chicken, and fish, with an accent on the organic. She is, however, as fearless at the range as her father is on the racetrack. In fact, Nell herself is a first-class driver in her own right, having completed the course required of all candidates for the circuit. Nell says some of her better recipes, which she had contributed to this book, have popped into her head while negotiating a tricky turn at 120 mph.

At present, Nell attends the College of the Atlantic in Maine, where she is pursuing ornithological studies with emphasis on the falcon, a bird that she has been studying for many years. You may be sure, however, that it will never wind up in one of her recipes.

URSULA HOTCHNER

Ursula Hotchner is a native of Cologne, Germany, and her culinary skills were once limited to the dishes of her own country. She makes a fantastic Rouladen (see page 66 for recipe). But when she went to live in Paris in 1971, she fell under the spell of French cooking. Ursula enrolled in the famed Cordon Bleu cooking school, where she labored over a hot stove all through that winter, eventually graduating with a diploma that certifies that she has mastered classical French cooking. During that period, her husband gained ten pounds.

But now, in deference to his waistline, she has adapted some of the Cordon Bleu dishes to today's preference for lighter foods, and these changes are reflected in the dishes she had contributed to the book. When the Newmans come to dinner, these are the dishes she cooks.

One of the secrets of her success in the kitchen is the fact that she raises a large garden of fresh vegetables, and maintains an extensive herb garden outside her kitchen door. These are both prey to marauding woodchucks and racoons, but since both Newman and Hotchner are herbal devotees and fiends for fresh vegetables, they spend a lot of time combatting the marauders by installing electric fences, night lights, scarecrows, and other devious devices. They considered hiding in the surrounding bushes with pellet guns but were afraid they'd shoot each other.

PART II
THE RECIPES

NEWMAN'S LAW

"The good thing about excesses is that you can't get too much of them."

P. L. Newman, 1985

APPETIZERS

I have two favorite appetizers. One is a dozen tiny clams on the half-shell, topped with a squirt of lemon juice and a dollop of fresh horseradish – but *never* that dread spicy-catsup cocktail sauce! If baby clams are not available, I'll settle for a plate of celery hearts chopped fine in an oil and vinegar dressing, which I concoct.

I like any kind of melon as a starter, even watermelon (although I'd rather have watermelon as dessert). I eat watermelon in very unlikely places, though, such as the sauna and the shower. (*PLN*)

SMOKED SALMON
AND ASPARAGUS

20–24 fresh asparagus spears
4 thin slices smoked salmon
Watercress sprigs for garnish
To taste:
    Extra-virgin olive oil
    Wine vinegar
    Freshly ground black pepper
    Capers

Cut all asparagus to about 6 inches long; steam or boil until al dente (tender-crisp), and cool by immediately immersing in cold water. Wrap smoked salmon around five or six spears to make bundles. Place an asparagus bundle on each plate; garnish with watercress. At the table, pass cruets of oil and vinegar, a pepper mill, and a small bowl of drained capers.

SERVES 4

CARPACCIO

1 pound beef filet
3–4 ounces Parmesan cheese, chipped
Juice from one lemon
2 tablespoons extra-virgin olive oil
Salt and freshly ground black pepper
Capers (optional)

Four hours prior to serving, place meat in freezer. Immediately before serving, remove and slice paper thin. Arrange slices on a large serving platter, distribute Parmesan over the meat, and sprinkle with lemon juice, olive oil, salt, pepper, and, if desired, capers.

SERVES 8

COLD SALMON MOUSSE

This is one of those appetizers that allow you to mingle with your guests before dinner since all you have to do is take it out of the refrigerator, unmold it, and serve it with crackers. It can also be served as a first course. (*UH*)

1 15-ounce can salmon
½ cup olive oil
2 tablespoons lemon juice
Freshly ground black pepper
Pinch salt
1½ cups very cold whipping cream

Drain and pick over salmon and crumble in a bowl. Add oil, lemon juice, pepper, and salt. Beat into the salmon until you've obtained a smooth, evenly blended mixture. Whip cream until stiff. Fold carefully into the salmon mixture until completely incorporated. Refrigerate in a 1-quart mold for at least 2 hours, but preferably not more than 24.

SERVES 10–12

CRABMEAT TIDBITS

½ cup mayonnaise
½ cup fresh or frozen crabmeat
3 minced shallots
1 cup grated Parmesan cheese
2 teaspoons curry powder
Salt and pepper
24–28 butter-flavored crackers

Combine mayonnaise, crabmeat, shallots, ¾ cup of Parmesan cheese, curry powder, and salt and pepper to taste, and mix well. Mound mixture on crackers, top with remaining Parmesan cheese, and brown lightly under broiler.

MAKES 24–28 TIDBITS

GUACAMOLE

2 avocados, mashed
2 tablespoons lime or lemon juice
1 clove garlic, finely minced
¼ cup red salsa (mild or hot, according to taste)
3 tablespoons Newman's Own salad dressing or
   Vinaigrette Dressing (see page 32 for recipe)
Salt and pepper

Combine all ingredients and mix well. Chill for 1–2 hours tightly covered. Serve with tortilla chips.

**SERVES 8
(MAKES ABOUT 2 CUPS)**

MARTHA STEWART'S VICTORIAN SAVOURIES

FILLING

½ small onion, chopped
3 tablespoons olive oil
3 tablespoons chopped fresh basil
Salt and pepper
1 tablespoon chopped fresh parsley

1 32-ounce jar Newman's Own
  marinara sauce or 1 quart of your
  favorite homemade marinara sauce
1 tablespoon drained tiny capers
Pinch cayenne pepper

Sauté the onion in olive oil until tender. Add remaining ingredients, including salt and pepper to taste. Bring to simmer and remove from heat.

PUFFS

1 pound puff pastry, homemade or
  store-bought (thawed if frozen)
1 egg yolk
2 tablespoons heavy cream

Preheat oven to 400°F. Roll the puff pastry into a rectangle ⅛ inch thick. Cut into 1½-inch squares with a pastry cutter. Place squares on an unbuttered baking sheet, 1 inch apart. Brush tops of the squares with egg glaze, made by mixing yolk and cream together. With a ¾-inch biscuit cutter, cut circle in center of each pastry square, but do not cut all the way through to the baking sheet. Bake for 10–12 minutes, until puffed and golden. Cool on rack. (Puffs can be frozen at this point for later use.)

To serve, warm puffs. With the point of a knife, remove the round of pastry from each. Fill the holes in the puffs with the above filling. Serve with a tiny sprig of parsley or chopped basil as garnish.

MAKES 200-250 PUFFS

19

NEWMAN'S LAW

"It is useless to put on your brakes when you are upside down."

P. L. Newman
to A. E. Hotchner at
the scene of the crash

20

SOUPS

TOMATO BISQUE WITH RICE

2 cups chopped onions
2 tablespoons butter or margarine
1 32-ounce jar Newman's Own spaghetti sauce *or*
    homemade spaghetti sauce
3 cups water
3 cups peeled and chopped fresh or canned tomatoes
1 tablespoon dried oregano
1 tablespoon dried basil *or* 2 tablespoons fresh basil
1½ cups milk
4–6 ounces Monterey Jack or medium-sharp
    cheddar cheese, grated
3 cups cooked brown rice
Salt and pepper

Sauté onion in butter until translucent. Add spaghetti sauce, water, tomatoes, oregano, and basil. Simmer 20 minutes. Turn heat to low so bisque barely bubbles. Stir in the milk, cheese, rice, and salt and pepper to taste. Serve when the cheese is melted.

SERVES 10–12

NELL NEWMAN'S CHICKEN SOUP

My father has an inexhaustible fondness for soups and often makes a quick-step chicken soup with a prepared mix that he combines with noodles and fresh vegetables. In fact, give my father a hearty soup, a can of beer, and a bag of popcorn, and he is as close to heaven as he can get.

He does handstands over my chicken soup, but in all fairness I must acknowledge that my recipe was inspired by the chicken soup that our English governess, Duffy, made for us when we were little girls.

1 plump (4–5 pounds) roasting chicken, cut into pieces
4 quarts cold water
1½ pounds carrots, chopped coarse
1 bunch celery, chopped coarse
2 medium leeks, chopped coarse
4 medium onions, chopped coarse
1 large bay leaf
1 cup fresh or frozen and thawed peas
1 cup fresh or frozen and thawed corn niblets
Chopped garlic
Beau Monde seasoning *or* a mixture of salt, instant
    dry onion, and celery seed
Freshly ground black pepper
Spike (optional; explanation follows)
Egg noodles

I cut a plump roasting chicken into pieces. I coarsely cut 1½ pounds of carrots and a bunch of celery. The other ingredients are 2 medium leeks, 4 medium onions, a large bay leaf, a cup of fresh or frozen peas, and a cup of corn niblets. I then add, to taste, garlic, Beau Monde (which contains salt, onion, and celery seed), ground black pepper, and spike, a mixture of assorted herbs and seaweed, a favorite ingredient of mine that is available in health food stores.

The day before I serve this dish to my father, I put the chicken pieces in 4 quarts of water, along with the onions, garlic to taste, leeks, bay leaf, and one-fourth of the amount of carrots and celery I have prepared. I bring this to a boil for 45 minutes, then simmer it for 3 hours, after which I allow it to cool. Only after it is completely cool do I remove and debone the chicken, thereby having allowed the juices to be reabsorbed. I then put the stock with the deboned chicken in the refrigerator overnight.

When I'm ready to prepare the dish for serving, I skim all the fat off the stock and bring the stock to a boil, adding the rest of the celery and carrots, the peas and corn, and the seasonings to taste. I then cook a generous amount of egg noodles in a separate pot. Of course, the dish is served in soup bowls, with the egg noodles served in a separate bowl so that each diner can determine the amount that he would like in his soup. I also serve a basket of hot garlic bread and grilled cheese sandwiches to accompany the soup.

SERVES 8–10

23

CURRIED CREAM OF BROCCOLI WITH RICE AND LENTILS

Serve this soup with bread and salad for a hearty meal. (*NN*)

1 large bunch broccoli, chopped, including stems
1 medium onion, chopped
6 cups chicken stock or ½ cup Vogue
   (see note below) added to 6 cups water
2–3 teaspoons curry powder
½ cup brown rice
½ cup red lentils
1½ cups water
1 cup cream or milk
Salt and pepper

Place broccoli and onion in pot with stock and curry. Simmer until tender. Meanwhile, wash rice and lentils and cook together with 1½ cups of water until rice is tender but chewy. Place small portions of broccoli and stock in a blender or food processor and puree. Place creamed soup in a different pot and add milk, rice and beans, and salt and pepper to taste. Reheat and serve.

Note: Vogue broths are chemical-free and preservative-free powdered broths that can be found in health food stores.

SERVES 10

CUCUMBER WATERCRESS SOUP

4–5 large cucumbers, peeled and halved
Large pinch salt
⅓ cup scallions, chopped
1 tablespoon dried dill *or*
    3 tablespoons fresh dill
½ cup watercress, large stems removed
White pepper
⅔ cup sour cream or more

Scrape cucumber seeds into a sieve set over a bowl, then sprinkle with salt and press out juices. Cut cucumber into chunks. In a processor, puree cucumber chunks and scallions, juice pressed out of seeds, dill, watercress, and pepper to taste. Add sour cream and correct seasoning to taste. Refrigerate at least 1 hour to blend flavors. Garnish with fresh dill, watercress, and a dollop of sour cream.

SERVES 5–6

JOANNE'S GAZPACHO

Joanne Woodward

2 cups leftover salad, which can include lettuce,
    tomato, cucumber, onion, pepper, etc.
2 cups Newman's Own spaghetti sauce or your
    favorite homemade spaghetti sauce
1 cup beef bouillon
Chopped cucumber, scallion, and tomato
    for garnish (optional)

Puree salad ingredients, spaghetti sauce, and bouillon together in blender or food processor. Add more bouillon if necessary to reach desired consistency. Refrigerate 1 hour and garnish with chopped cucumber, scallion, and tomato if desired.

SERVES 4–6

26

CREAMY JERUSALEM ARTICHOKE AND RED PEPPER SOUP

Jerusalem artichokes are those bumpy-looking potatolike roots in the produce department of your neighborhood grocery store. If you are a brave soul who enjoys unusual foods, this recipe will definitely suit you. The soup is naturally very sweet and tastes almost exactly like artichokes, a vegetable I enjoy tremendously. Serve it with bread and salad for a light lunch or dinner. (*NN*)

6 cups scrubbed and cubed Jerusalem artichokes
4 cups homemade vegetable or chicken stock *or* ½ cup Vogue added to 4 cups water
2 cups chopped onion

4 tablespoons butter
1 cup chopped red bell pepper
2 cups cooked brown rice
2 cups milk or light cream
Salt and pepper

Place Jerusalem artichoke cubes and stock in pot set over low to medium heat. Simmer until tender, 30–45 minutes. Meanwhile, sauté the onion in butter until translucent, then add the red pepper and cook for 2–3 minutes. Remove from heat. Transfer small batches of artichokes and stock to the blender and combine until smooth. Place soup in another pot set over low heat and add rice, cream, salt and pepper to taste, and sautéed vegetables; heat through before serving.

SERVES 10–12

27

CAULIFLOWER AND PARMESAN SOUP WITH ESSENCE OF LEMON

This is a fantastically fresh, slightly lemony soup with new green peas (not canned) for color. It goes very well with Sesame Loaves (see page 88). This soup originated during one of my refrigerator-cleaning sprees, in which I throw all of my leftovers into a pot, heat them, and see what happens. (*NN*)

1 large head cauliflower, cut
   into 1-inch pieces
1 medium onion, chopped
6 cups chicken or vegetable stock
   or ½ cup Vogue stock added
   to 6 cups water

1 cup uncooked millet
2¼ cups water
⅓ cup grated Parmesan cheese
Juice of ½ lemon
1 cup fresh peas
Salt and pepper

Place cauliflower in a pot along with the onion and 6 cups of stock. Simmer over medium heat until tender. While cauliflower is cooking, wash the millet in a strainer, put into pot along with 2¼ cups water, and cook over medium heat until soft and fluffy. (This may require a bit more water.) When the cauliflower is cooked, place small batches in a blender or food processor along with the stock. Blend each batch until smooth and return to low heat. Add Parmesan cheese, lemon juice, millet, peas, and salt and pepper to taste. Mix well and warm for 5 minutes before serving.

SERVES 8–10

MELISSA'S MINESTRONE

Melissa Newman

1 large onion, chopped
1 stalk celery, chopped
1 carrot, chopped
¼ head green cabbage, shredded
¼ pound dried lima beans or kidney beans,
　　soaked overnight and cooked until tender
¼ pound fresh peas
3 cups water (more if needed)
1–2 chicken or vegetable bouillon cubes
2 cups Newman's Own spaghetti sauce
　　or your favorite homemade spaghetti sauce

Simmer vegetables in water and bouillon until tender, about 12–15 minutes. Add spaghetti sauce and simmer gently 5 minutes longer.

SERVES 8

29

NEWMAN'S LAW

"Whenever I do something good, right away I've got to do something bad, so I know I'm not going to pieces."

P. L. Newman, 1985

SALADS

Some people have sexual dreams, but I dream about food. Then, when I wake up, I want to eat the food I dreamed about. That means I have to keep a big pantry, because you never know.

This morning I didn't eat anything because I dreamed about liver last night and I hate liver.

My salad dressing is literally something I dreamed up, the main part of it in a long night's sleep; the adjustments came in short afternoon naps. (*PLN*)

31

TOMATO AND ENDIVE SALAD

I like salads for lunch, and this one is at the top of my list. Of course, I use Newman's Own dressing on them, but if you have the questionable taste of preferring some others, suit yourself. (*PLN*)

2 large, fresh, ripe tomatoes
½ pound endives
3 slices bacon

Newman's Own salad dressing *or* Vinaigrette Dressing (see following recipe)

Cut tomatoes into small dice. Slice endives to make an equal amount and mix with tomatoes. Cook bacon until very crisp. Crumble and sprinkle over salad. Toss with salad dressing to taste.

SERVES 4

VINAIGRETTE DRESSING

Any oil and vinegar (vinaigrette) dressing can be used in the recipes in this book that call for Newman's Own.

To make a basic vinaigrette, mix 1 part vinegar or lemon juice with 3 parts oil, then salt and pepper and add Dijon mustard to taste. Use extra-virgin olive oil and high-quality white or red wine vinegar for the best results; vary the ratio of oil to vinegar for a sharper or milder dressing. You may add garlic (chopped or a whole peeled clove for subtle flavoring), dried or fresh herbs, or other seasonings. For variety try an herb vinegar in place of plain wine vinegar.

MANDARIN CHICKEN SALAD

I serve this dish every year at our annual tennis luncheon, preparing it before the guests arrive, and I'm able to play a set of tennis while it bides its time in the fridge. (*UH*)

> 1 roasting chicken (4–5 pounds), poached and cooled
> 1 11-ounce can Mandarin orange segments
> 3 ounces fresh bean sprouts
> 4 ounces fresh mushrooms, sliced
> 1 cup frozen peas
> Soy sauce
> Newman's Own salad dressing *or*
>   Vinaigrette Dressing (see page 32 for recipe)

Remove chicken meat from the bones and cut into small pieces. Add orange segments, bean sprouts, mushrooms, and peas. Mix soy sauce to taste with salad dressing. Pour over chicken mixture and toss well. Refrigerate before serving.

SERVES 4

JOAN RIVERS' SHRIMP SALAD

2 pounds shrimp, cooked, shelled, and deveined
2 stalks celery, chopped
¼ cup chopped scallions or chives
2 tablespoons fresh or dried dill
½ cup Newman's Own salad dressing *or* Vinaigrette Dressing (see page 32 for recipe)
Lettuce
Tomato wedges

Mix shrimp, celery, scallions or chives, dill, and salad dressing. Chill in refrigerator for 1 hour or longer. Serve on bed of lettuce garnished with tomato wedges.

SERVES 4

CUCUMBER SALAD

The amount of each vegetable used really isn't important here, though cucumbers should dominate the other flavors. I've found that all salads taste better if the salad leaves are washed and put in the refrigerator in a damp towel about an hour before serving to allow them to get crisp and cold. The salad plates should also be put in the refrigerator. (*PLN*)

Thinly sliced cucumbers (wafer thin), peeled if waxed
Diced ripe tomatoes
Chopped romaine lettuce
Cubed red bell peppers
Cubed green bell peppers
Newman's Own salad dressing *or* Vinaigrette Dressing (see page 32 for recipe)

Toss the vegetables in a bowl with salad dressing to taste. Serve on chilled plates

34

CRISPY CHÈVRE SALAD

This is my version of a salad I was served in a little Paris restaurant. By varying the kind of chèvre you use, you can vary the taste. I prefer a piquant chèvre that contrasts sharply with the delicate flavors of the salad ingredients underneath (*UH*)

> 8 slices cylindrical chèvre, ⅓ inch
>   thick, without rind, chilled
> 1 egg, beaten
> ⅓ cup fresh bread crumbs
> Oil for deep frying
> Bibb lettuce
> Watercress
> Red leaf lettuce
> Vinaigrette Dressing (see page 32 for recipe)

Dip Chèvre wheels in egg, drain, and roll in bread crumbs, patting crumbs well to cover all surfaces of cheese. Refrigerate until ready to use. Deep fry in hot oil very quickly until deep golden. (Cheese must not become too warm or coating will split.) Tear greens into bite-size pieces and toss with vinaigrette to taste. Arrange 2 slices chèvre on each serving.

SERVES 4

CAROLINE MURPHY'S
TUNA SALAD

This is another one of my favorites and just one of our housekeeper's triumphs. I like it as a sandwich on Sesame Loaves (see page 88 for recipe). (*PLN*)

1 6½-ounce can tuna
1 teaspoon mustard
1 whole sweet pickle, minced
3 tablespoons mayonnaise
3 scallions, chopped fine
1 tablespoon sweet pickle juice

Drain tuna and flake into a bowl. Add remaining ingredients and mix well. Serve as a salad or sandwich filling.

SERVES 2–3

The *Guide Michelin* has awarded Newman four stars for his chicken pieces and five stars for his hat.

P. L. Newman, chicken fancier, preparing fancy chicken.

Newman may be chicken outside his car, but never behind the wheel.

The master preparing
his Hamburger-Pasta-
Broccoli Casserole
(see page 63 for
recipe).

What's sauce for the
goose is sauce for the
hamburger.

"Who the heck
cooked this burger?"
the crew chief
demanded.

Newman always takes
the first bite in case
there is not enough to
go around.

Until filled with Hamburger-
Pasta-Broccoli Casserole,
Newman's racing crew will not
fill his tyres with air.

That ecstatic
moment when
Newman has
sprinkled his
dressing on a salad
of his concoction:
preparing for "the
toss".

Newman won a gold for
his salad toss in the 1984
Olympics.

BROWN RICE SALAD

Sandy Falconer

Joanne is particularly fond of this dish because of the whole-grain base. It goes beautifully with Caroline's Southern Fried Chicken (see page 57 for recipe).

1 pound brown rice
Juice and zest of 1 orange
3 scallions, sliced thin crosswise

1½ pounds red or green seedless grapes, stemmed
5 ounces whole almonds, toasted

DRESSING

½ ounce fresh gingerroot, peeled
1½ tablespoons cider vinegar
1½ tablespoons brown sugar
2 tablespoons champagne vinegar
½ cup olive oil
½ cup vegetable oil

⅛ teaspoon ground nutmeg
1 teaspoon freshly ground black pepper
2 tablespoons coriander, toasted and ground
Salt

Blend dressing ingredients in food processor or blender until emulsified.

Boil rice in salted water until tender. Drain immediately. Add dressing, orange juice and zest, and scallions. Cool. Adjust seasonings to taste and add more vegetable or olive oil if needed. Fold in grapes and almonds and toss well.

SERVES 6–10

NEWMAN'S LAW

"You can get straight A's in marketing and still flunk ordinary life."

P. L. Newman to Lee Iacocca
after his Pinto caught fire

FISH AND SEAFOOD

JOANNE WOODWARD'S
SOLE CABERNET

At the top of my list of favorite dishes is Joanne's Sole Cabernet, which is in a class by itself. (*PLN*)

4 tablespoons butter
4 filets of sole
Salt and pepper
2 shallots
2 cups Cabernet Sauvignon
1 cup Joanne's Hollandaise Sauce
(see following recipe)

Put lumps of butter on the filets of sole and fold them over crosswise. Add salt and pepper to taste and the shallots. Place in baking pan and add 2 cups good Cabernet Sauvignon. Bake in 375° F oven for 10 minutes, remove the fish, pour the sauce into a saucepan, and reduce the sauce to one-third its original amount. Let cool; add Joanne's Hollandaise Sauce to the sauce before returning the sole and the sauce to the baking pan. Place in oven for 5 minutes and serve.

SERVES 4

JOANNE'S HOLLANDAISE SAUCE

3 egg yolks
3 tablespoons cold water
8 tablespoons lightly salted butter, melted

Pepper
Juice of ½ lemon

Place egg yolks and water in top of double boiler over hot but not boiling water. Stir with wooden spoon until mixture thickens. Remove from heat. Add butter, little by little, while stirring. Add pepper to taste. Just before serving, add lemon juice.

MAKES 2 CUPS

DILLED FILETS OF SCROD À LA NEWMAN

Coming in a distant second to Joanne's Sole Cabernet is my own dilled filet of scrod, which I bake in the oven, liberally coating it with lots of fresh dill, butter, and lemon juice. (*PLN*)

2 pounds scrod filets
3–4 tablespoons fresh dill *or*
   1 tablespoon dried dill
½ cup (1 stick) butter

¾ cup dry white wine
1 cup Joanne's Hollandaise Sauce
   (see recipe above)

Preheat oven to 375° F. Wash and dry filets. Arrange in single layer in 13″ × 9″ × 2″ baking dish. Cover with fresh dill or sprinkle with dried dill. Heat butter and wine together in small saucepan until butter melts. Pour over fish. Bake for 20 minutes or just until fish separates easily when touched with a fork. Serve with Joanne's Hollandaise Sauce.

SERVES 4

ITALIAN BAKED SCROD

This is really a variation on the preceding recipe, but the resulting flavor is so different that it deserves a name of its own. (*PLN*)

2 pounds scrod filets
Salt
Pepper
Sliced onions
Chopped stewed tomatoes
Sliced pitted ripe olives

2 tablespoons chopped fresh basil *or*
    1 tablespoon dried basil
2 tablespoons chopped fresh parsley *or*
    1 tablespoon dried parsley
1 clove garlic, crushed
Clam juice

Wash and dry filets. Arrange in single layer in 13″ × 9″ × 2″ baking dish. Season with salt and pepper to taste. Cover filets with onions, tomatoes, olives, basil, parsley, and garlic. Moisten with a little clam juice and bake in preheated 375° F oven for 20 minutes or just until fish separates easily when touched with a fork. Drain off most of the liquid before serving.

SERVES 4

SPANISH SWORDFISH

Hemingway and I used to eat at a little restaurant on the beach at Torremolinas in southernmost Spain, run by an old Basque fisherman. We were so smitten by this swordfish that I asked the old man to show me how to cook it. I once tried to cook it on a grill in Ketchum, Idaho, but the swordfish was frozen and had no taste. Now I often show it off in Connecticut when the local fish store alerts me to a swordfish fresh off the hook. (*AEH*)

2 pounds 2-inch-thick swordfish
   steak, cut evenly
1 cup Newman's Own salad dressing
   or Vinaigrette Dressing
   (see page 32 for recipe)
¼ cup lime juice

1 tablespoon dried thyme *or*
   rosemary *or* 3 tablespoons
   fresh thyme or rosemary
Lemon juice
Butter

Marinate swordfish in salad dressing, lime juice, and thyme or rosemary for several hours. Prepare charcoal and place fish on the grill when coals are gray. Saturate with lemon juice, chunks of butter, and more thyme and cook 10 minutes on each side. Turn only once, basting with more lemon juice and marinade and dotting with butter after turning. Remove fish, place a freshly cut pine bough on fire, put fish on top of pine bough, and let it be seared by the flame. Remove immediately after the pine flame dies down and serve.

SERVES 4–6

NELL'S CRAB CAKES

3 pounds fresh or frozen crabmeat
2 eggs
4 cups fine bread crumbs
4 tablespoons mustard
1 cup mayonnaise
1 cup chopped onion
2 cups chopped celery
⅔ cup finely chopped cilantro or parsley
Salt and pepper

Pick the cartilage from crabmeat and combine crabmeat with all other ingredients, including salt and pepper to taste. (I've found that this is best done with the hands, as the mixture is rather thick.) When thoroughly blended, form into burger-size patties (cakes should be tightly formed so they do not fall apart), wrap in wax paper, and chill until ready to use.

Crab cakes may be deep fried, but they are best when placed on greased tinfoil and broiled until browned on both sides. Great with or without tartar sauce.

MAKES ABOUT 20

HERBED RED SNAPPER

This dish is guaranteed to make your guests' eyes sparkle because it looks as good as it tastes. (*UH*)

1 whole red snapper (3–4 pounds)
Fresh or dried dill and thyme
4 tablespoons butter
Salt and pepper
1 bunch watercress
Joanne's Hollandaise Sauce
   (see page 40 for recipe) or lemon butter
Cherry tomatoes *or* sliced tomatoes and
   quartered hard-boiled eggs for garnish

Place the whole fish in a well-greased casserole. Sprinkle dill and thyme over the fish and dot with half the butter and salt and pepper to taste. Broil 4–6 inches from the oven's heat source about 10 minutes on each side, dotting with remaining butter after turning the fish. Serve on a bed of watercress with lemon butter or Joanne's Hollandaise Sauce. Garnish with cherry tomatoes or sliced tomatoes and quartered hard-boiled eggs.

SERVES 4

SPINACH/MUSHROOM-STUFFED FILET OF SOLE

10 ounces frozen and thawed chopped spinach *or*
  fresh spinach, washed
1 tablespoon minced shallots
4 ounces mushrooms, chopped fine
1 tablespoon olive oil
2/3 cup ricotta cheese
3 ounces cream cheese, softened
3 tablespoons grated Parmesan cheese
1 egg
1/2 teaspoon dry mustard
1/8 teaspoon ground nutmeg
Salt and pepper
6–8 filets of sole
6–8 teaspoons dry sherry

Sauté spinach in a dry pan until water has evaporated. Cool. Sauté shallots and mushrooms in olive oil until liquid has evaporated. Mix with spinach and cool.

In a bowl, combine cheeses, egg, and spices, including salt and pepper to taste. Mix in the cooked spinach/mushroom mixture.

Spread a teaspoon of dry sherry on each filet, then spread 1/2–1/3 cup of filling on each and roll up gently. Bake at 350° F about 20–30 minutes.

SERVES 6–8

BROILER MARINATED SCALLOPS

½ cup (1 stick) butter or margarine
1 pound scallops
1 teaspoon soy sauce
2–4 tablespoons chopped fresh basil
3 tablespoons Newman's Own salad dressing *or*
    Vinaigrette Dressing (see page 32 for recipe)
Salt and pepper

Melt butter and remove from heat. Add remaining ingredients, including salt and pepper to taste, and mix well. Refrigerate for 1–4 hours in baking dish. Place in preheated oven about 4–6 inches from heat source and broil until lightly browned (about 5–10 minutes, depending on whether you use the small bay scallops or larger sea scallops). Remove and serve with brown rice, if desired.

SERVES 2–3

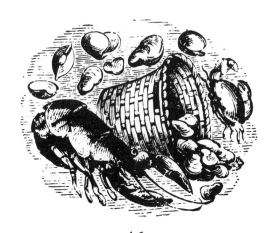

JOANNE'S CIOPPINO

Joanne Woodward

¼ cup salad or olive oil
2 cloves garlic, minced
2 medium onions, chopped
2 green peppers, seeded and chopped
1 32-ounce jar Newman's Own spaghetti sauce *or*
    1 quart of your favorite homemade spaghetti sauce
1 cup dry white wine
1½ pounds cod, sliced and cut into pieces
8 ounces frozen lobster tails, thawed,
    shelled, and cut up
1 pound mussels and/or small clams

Heat oil in a deep, heavy skillet or Dutch oven; add garlic, onions, and green peppers. Cook until golden. Add spaghetti sauce, wine, cod, and lobster; simmer 6 minutes. Add mussels and/or clams. Cover and cook 5 minutes more, until fish is done and shellfish open.

Serve this seafood stew with crusty Italian bread. To round out the meal, add a salad of romaine lettuce with slivers of cheese and walnuts, tossed with Newman's Own salad dressing or with your favorite vinaigrette (see page 32 for a recipe).

SERVES 6

NEWMAN'S LAW

*"Just when things look
darkest they go black."*

P. L. Newman to
Walter Mondale, 1984

48

POULTRY

The Hotchners raise pedigree chickens of exotic mien, as witness their cochon rooster, who is posing with Newman in the first color section. These exotic fowl are raised only for their eggs and not for the chopping block. The difference between using fresh eggs right out of the henhouse and using store-bought eggs is the difference between fresh and frozen foods. The Araucana hens even lay beautiful colored eggs of blue-green shades from turquoise to deep olive, which are very popular around Easter time.

As for chicken itself, a favorite with both the Newmans and the Hotchners is chicken breasts cooked on the outdoor grill with the cover closed, which creates the uniform heat of an oven and flavors the breasts with charcoal-laced smoke. It is important that the breasts be basted during the cooking process, and of course both Paul and Hotch use their salad dressing for this purpose. In fact, they marinate the breasts in the salad dressing overnight before cooking them.

For everyday indoor cooking, here are various poultry recipes that are family favorites.

CHICKEN WITH ROSEMARY

Fresh rosemary is the key ingredient in this dish; don't substitute the dried herb. (*NN*)

1½ pounds skinned and boned chicken breasts, cut into bite-size pieces
5 tablespoons butter, plus butter to sauté chicken
½ cup minced onions
¼ pound mushrooms, sliced
3 tablespoons flour
⅓ cup chicken broth
⅓ cup dry white wine

½ cup light cream
1 8-ounce can artichoke hearts (in brine, not oil), cut into bite-size pieces
⅓ cup freshly grated Parmesan cheese
1½–2 tablespoons minced fresh rosemary
Salt and pepper

Sauté chicken pieces quickly in some butter. Don't cook through; just sear outside to seal in juices. Set aside.

Melt 2 tablespoons butter in pan and in it sauté onions and mushrooms until onions are limp. Add remaining 3 tablespoons butter and, after butter has melted, stir in flour. Stir a minute or so. Add broth and wine and stir well. Add cream and cook over low heat, stirring, until sauce is thick. Add artichoke hearts, Parmesan, rosemary, and salt and pepper to taste.

About 10–15 minutes before serving, stir the chicken into the sauce. Don't overcook or chicken will be dry. It should be very tender and moist. You may want to add some more broth if the mixture is too thick. Serve over noodles or rice.

SERVES 3–4

CHICKEN AND MARINATED ARTICHOKE HEARTS EN CASSEROLE

2 cups drained canned artichoke hearts
Newman's Own salad dressing *or*
   Vinaigrette Dressing (see page 32 for recipe)
3 cups diced skinned and boned chicken breasts
2 tablespoons butter
¼ cup vermouth, dry sherry, or dry white wine
Salt and pepper
1½ cups grated medium-sharp cheddar
4 tablespoons freshly grated Parmesan cheese

Marinate canned artichoke hearts in salad dressing for 2 hours prior to preparation of dish. Then drain and quarter the artichokes.

Sauté diced chicken in butter for 3 minutes. Add wine and salt and pepper to taste. Continue cooking until chicken pieces are barely white all over. Place chicken in a baking dish along with artichoke hearts and cover with cheeses. Place in preheated 350° F oven for 30 minutes or until cheese is brown and bubbly.

Serve on buttered spinach noodles or egg noodles.

SERVES 4

CHICKEN PARMESAN

3 whole skinned and boned chicken breasts, halved
2 eggs, lightly beaten
1 cup seasoned flour
   (use salt, pepper, and other herbs if desired)
1–2 cups freshly grated Parmesan cheese
3 tablespoons butter or margarine
1 large onion, chopped
1 32-ounce jar Newman's Own spaghetti sauce *or*
   1 quart homemade spaghetti sauce
2 cups grated mozzarella cheese

Dip chicken breasts in egg, dredge in the seasoned flour, and roll in Parmesan, forcing cheese into all of the nooks and crannies.

Place chicken in frying pan with butter and brown on both sides (about 3–5 minutes a side). Remove and place in baking dish. Cover chicken with chopped onion, spaghetti sauce, mozzarella, and any leftover Parmesan. Bake at 350° F until browned on top, about 30 minutes.

SERVES 6

TORTELLINI WITH CHICKEN

Gay Talese

1 medium onion, chopped
2 tablespoons butter
3 skinned and boned chicken breast halves,
  cut into 2-inch pieces
Salt and pepper
1 tablespoon dried tarragon or thyme *or*
  2 tablespoons fresh tarragon or thyme (optional)
Flour for dredging
2–3 cups Newman's Own spaghetti sauce *or*
  homemade spaghetti sauce
10 ounces cheese or meat tortellini, prepared
  according to package directions
Chopped parsley for garnish

Sauté onion in butter until limp and set aside. Season chicken with salt and pepper to taste and tarragon if desired. Dredge in flour and sauté in pan used to sauté onion for about 5–7 minutes. Add onions, spaghetti sauce, and tortellini. Stir together, heating thoroughly for 5–10 minutes. Garnish with parsley.

SERVES 4

CHICKEN MARINARA

I cook dinner on Mother's Day, and of all my dishes this is the one that earned me the most Papa points. (*AEH*)

    4 large skinned and boned chicken breast portions
    4 tablespoons butter or oil
    1 small onion, diced
    1 pound fresh spinach or 1 package frozen chopped spinach
    ¼ cup ricotta cheese
    2 tablespoons freshly grated Parmesan cheese
    ⅛ teaspoon ground nutmeg
    1 32-ounce jar Newman's Own spaghetti sauce with mushrooms
       or 1 quart of your favorite homemade spaghetti sauce
       with sautéed sliced mushrooms added to taste.
    8 ounces spinach noodles or linguine

Form a pocket in the underside of each chicken breast, where bone was removed, for stuffing. Heat 2 tablespoons butter or oil and sauté onion in it until golden. Wash and stem spinach if fresh and cook in water that clings to leaves, about 2 minutes to wilt. Drain well and chop. If using frozen spinach, thaw and drain well. Combine with onion in pan. Remove from heat and add cheeses and nutmeg. Stuff a few tablespoons of mixture in each chicken breast. Fold the ends of the chicken under to enclose the filling. Spread remaining butter or oil in a baking dish and arrange chicken pieces, stuffed side down, in dish. Pour spaghetti sauce with mushrooms over chicken. Place in preheated 350° F oven and bake 45–50 minutes. Cook noodles and serve with chicken breasts, spooning sauce over all.

SERVES 4

P. LOQUESTO'S CHICKEN CREOLE

I dreamed up this recipe while driving at Malibu Race Track. (*PLN*)

1 medium onion, chopped
1 green pepper, chopped
1 tablespoon vegetable oil
2 cups diced cooked chicken
1 cup cooked rice
2 cups Newman's Own spaghetti sauce *or*
    homemade spaghetti sauce
Dash ground nutmeg.

Sauté onion and pepper in oil until limp. Add chicken, rice, spaghetti sauce, and nutmeg. Simmer, covered, over low heat for 45 minutes or bake at 350° F for 45 minutes.

SERVES 4–5

HOTCH POTCH

You can actually throw anything that's handy into the pan and it will fit right in with this dish. (*AEH*)

4 medium potatoes, peeled, quartered, and parboiled
3 tablespoons cooking oil
1½ pounds chicken breasts, skinned, boned,
   and cut into bite-size pieces
3 tablespoons butter or margarine
1 medium onion, chopped coarse
1 stalk celery, chopped coarse
1 green pepper, seeded and chopped coarse
1 red pepper, seeded and chopped coarse
2 medium tomatoes, peeled and chopped
Pepper
Worcestershire sauce
¼ cup soy sauce

In a heavy pan, brown potatoes well in half the oil. Remove and set aside. Brown chicken pieces in the same pan, reduce heat, and continue cooking, stirring occasionally. While chicken is cooking, go on to vegetables.

In a separate pan set over medium-high heat, sauté onions and celery in butter or margarine until golden. Add the peppers and toss and shake for about 1 minute. Add tomatoes, pepper and Worcestershire sauce to taste, and soy sauce. Simmer 1–2 minutes and add chicken and potatoes. Stir together and serve.

SERVES 4

CAROLINE'S
SOUTHERN FRIED CHICKEN

Our housekeeper, Caroline Murphy, has taken several of the dishes she sets on our table and contributed them to this book. Her Ham Hocks and Beans is one of my all-time favorites, her Tuna Salad is unmatched (see pages 36 and 68 for recipes), and her Southern Fried Chicken is out of this world. (*PLN*)

> 1 fryer (about 3 pounds), cut up
> Sea salt
> Paprika
> Herbamare or Spike (see below)
> 2 cups vegetable oil

Season chicken well and set aside for 1 hour to let seasonings penetrate the chicken.

Heat oil to very hot and fry the chicken 12–15 minutes on each side. Keep lid on to prevent splattering and help chicken cook faster.

Note: Spike is a health food seasoning – a mixture of assorted herbs and seaweed explained in Nell's Chicken Soup (see page 22).

SERVES 2–3

COQ AU VIN

8–12 small white onions
2 tablespoons butter
4–6 ounces salt pork, diced
1 roasting chicken, cut up
Flour for dredging
Salt and pepper
¼ cup cognac
2–3 cups Burgundy or Beaujolais

1–2 cups beef bouillon
¼ teaspoon dried thyme
1 bay leaf
1 tablespoon tomato paste
2 cloves garlic, peeled and
  crushed
8 ounces mushrooms, sliced and
  sautéed in a little butter

In a heavy pan or casserole, brown onions well in the butter. Remove and set aside. Boil salt pork for about 10 minutes, drain, pat dry, and sauté in the pan until lightly browned. Remove and set aside. Dredge chicken in flour and brown in the fat/butter. Season with salt and pepper to taste. Add cognac, ignite, and shake pan until flame subsides. Return onions and salt pork to the pan with the chicken. Pour in the wine and enough bouillon to cover the chicken. Add thyme, bay leaf, tomato paste, and garlic. Stir well and simmer covered about 30–40 minutes or until chicken is done. (If you desire a thicker sauce, remove chicken, pork, and onion and whisk a paste of 1½ tablespoons butter and 2 tablespoons flour into the wine/bouillon sauce.) Arrange chicken, pork, and onions in a serving casserole, add sautéed mushrooms, and pour sauce over all. Serve with parsleyed potatoes.

SERVES 4–6

URSULA'S CORNISH HENS

4 Cornish hens
Salt and pepper
2 tablespoons dried tarragon *or*
   4–5 tablespoons fresh tarragon
1 medium onion, chopped
1 stalk celery, chopped
1 carrot, chopped
6 tablespoons butter
1 cup chicken broth
½ cup white wine
½ cup heavy cream

Place hens, seasoned with salt and pepper to taste and tarragon, in large well-greased pan. Surround with the chopped vegetables and dot butter over all. Roast in 425° F oven until done, about 50 minutes. Remove hens and keep warm. Skim fat from casserole. Add broth and wine and reduce over medium-high heat, stirring well, until slightly thickened. Add cream and simmer 2–3 minutes to blend flavors. Strain sauce and serve with hens.

SERVES 4

NEWMAN'S LAW

"There are three rules for running a business; unfortunately, we don't know any of them."

P. L. Newman to
A. E. Hotchner
during a lie detector test

MEAT
BEEF

URSULA'S POT ROAST

2# 4–5 pounds rump roast
2 tablespoons oil
4 medium onions, quartered
2 tablespoons flour
2 cups bouillon
2 cups red wine
1 tablespoon tomato paste
2 bay leaves
1 tablespoon dried thyme *or*
   3 tablespoons fresh thyme
1 tablespoon dried rosemary *or*
   3 tablespoons fresh rosemary
Salt and pepper

Brown roast in oil on all sides, remove, and set aside. Brown onions in the same oil, remove, and reserve. Add flour and cook until dark brown and well blended. Add bouillon, wine, and tomato paste. Cook and stir until thickened. Return roast and onions to pot and add bay leaves, thyme, rosemary, and salt and pepper to taste. Cover and place in 350°F oven for 3 hours. Serve with small new potatoes and carrots.

SERVES 6–8

61

THE NEWMANBURGER

Ground chuck
Vegetable oil
Hamburger buns

Sliced tomatoes
Thinly sliced Bermuda onion
Slivered kosher dill pickles

Don't make the mistake of using ground round or sirloin in this recipe; many hamburger cooks fall short of my standards because they use meat that is simply too good. I cook all my hamburgers on the outdoor grill or the indoor fireplace grill, and chuck is best suited to a hot charcoal fire.

Form the chuck into hamburger patties of the preferred size. I toss them from hand to hand to keep them fluffy. Never pat down the meat or the hamburger won't be able to breathe while it's cooking. Also, never put salt, pepper, or any other seasoning in the meat before cooking because that will toughen it. The idea of adding onions, eggs, bread crumbs, or any other ingredient to the meat raises my hackles. Never confuse steak tartare with the pure hamburger.

Prepare the charcoal and grease the grill with vegetable oil, but don't put the meat on the fire until the charcoal is a uniform grayish-white. Sear the burgers well on one side and turn them only once. After turning them, lower the grill for a brief time to sear the meat. The result: a hamburger that is crisp on the outside, tomato-red inside.

While the Newmanburgers are cooking, toast the buns around the edge of the grill. At my house, tomatoes, sliced onions, and pickles are the inevitable accompaniments. If corn is in season, it is also made part of the meal, always cooked for precisely 3 minutes and not a second longer in boiling, sweetened water. And a huge salad bowl, brimming with whatever fresh makings the market has to offer, is the table's centerpiece.

Although the Newmanburger is usually accompanied by frosty mugs of beer, on occasional impulse I serve up a bottle of 1962 Mouton-Rothschild or its equivalent, and that's when the Newmanburger tastes its best! (*PLN*)

HAMBURGER-PASTA-BROCCOLI CASSEROLE

4 cups Newman's Own spaghetti
  sauce or homemade spaghetti
  sauce
1 teaspoon salt
½ teaspoon pepper
2 pounds ground lean chuck

1 bunch broccoli, trimmed
  and cut into flowerets
1 16-ounce box spiral-shaped
  pasta
⅓ cup grated Parmesan cheese

Combine ¼ cup of the spaghetti sauce, the salt, pepper, and beef in medium-size bowl. Mix lightly to blend well. Shape into 8 equal patties. Sauté in large skillet in their own fat over medium heat until patties are cooked to desired doneness.

Steam broccoli just until fork tender, 3–4 minutes; do not overcook. Drain.

Cook pasta in large pot of boiling salted water until al dente, just tender; do not overcook. Drain.

Heat remaining spaghetti sauce in medium-size saucepan just until bubbly.

Arrange burgers, broccoli, and pasta in alternating layers in 3-quart casserole. Spoon the sauce over all. Sprinkle with grated Parmesan. Baked in preheated 375°F oven for 15–20 minutes or until hot and bubbly.

SERVES 8

NELL'S CHILI CON CARNE

2 cups diced onion
3 cloves garlic, minced
1 green pepper, seeded and chopped
2 tablespoons cooking oil
2 pounds coarsely ground lean beef
2 cups kidney beans, soaked overnight
1 32-ounce jar Newman's Own spaghetti sauce *or*
   1 quart of your favorite homemade spaghetti sauce
2–3 cups water
2–3 tablespoons chili powder
1 teaspoon ground cumin
Salt and pepper
1 cup chopped celery
1 7- or 8-ounce can corn
Sour cream and lime wedges for garnish

Sauté onion, garlic, and pepper in oil until soft. Add beef and brown. Add kidney beans, spaghetti sauce, water, chili powder, cumin, and salt and pepper to taste. Simmer, uncovered, 1 hour, stirring frequently. Add celery and corn and simmer 1 more hour. Garnish with sour cream and lime wedges.

Note: Substitute 3 cups cooked rice for the meat to make vegetarian chili.

SERVES 8

COLOGNE ROULADEN

This recipe was passed on to me by my mother, who learned it from my grandmother. (*UH*)

> 8 thin slices top round beef
> Mustard
> 1 tablespoon dried rosemary *or*
>   3 tablespoons fresh rosemary
> 1 tablespoon dried thyme *or*
>   3 tablespoons fresh thyme
> Salt and pepper
> 2 medium onions, quartered
> 2 dill pickles, quartered lengthwise
> 4 slices bacon, halved
> Flour for dredging
> 3 tablespoons oil or bacon fat
> 2 cups dry red wine
> 2 cups beef bouillon

Spread slices of beef with mustard and sprinkle with rosemary, thyme, and salt and pepper to taste. Place an onion quarter, a pickle quarter, and half a slice of bacon on each slice of beef. Roll up and secure each with 3 toothpicks. Dredge beef rolls in flour and brown them in oil or bacon fat in an ovenproof casserole over medium-high heat. Add wine and bouillon. Cover, reduce heat, and simmer slowly for 2 hours. Serve each person 2 rolls.

SERVES 4

LAMB

LAMB STEW

3 pounds boneless lamb shoulder, cut into 2-inch cubes
Salt and pepper
3 tablespoons olive oil
1 tablespoon butter
1 carrot, sliced
2 medium onions, chopped
3 tablespoons flour
3 cups rich beef broth
1 cup white wine
1 16-ounce can plum tomatoes, drained and chopped
2 cloves garlic, mashed

2 teaspoons dried rosemary or 1½ tablespoons fresh rosemary
1 teaspoon dried thyme or 1 tablespoon fresh thyme
1 bay leaf
¾ pound small white onions, peeled
¾ pound peeled baby potatoes or regular potatoes, peeled, quartered, and cut into small balls or ovals with melon baller
¾ pound baby carrots
1½ cups frozen peas
⅓ pound snow peas

Season lamb with salt and pepper to taste. In a heavy pan or casserole, brown lamb well in olive oil and butter over high heat. Remove meat. Lower heat to medium and brown sliced carrot and chopped onions until golden. Return lamb and juices to pan and sprinkle flour over meat. Stir well and cook 2 minutes. Add broth and wine, stirring and scraping all particles off the bottom of the pan. Add tomatoes, garlic, and herbs and simmer or bake at 350°F for about 1 hour or until lamb is tender. Add small white onions, potatoes, and baby carrots and cook 10–15 minutes more. Blanch peas and snow peas for 1 minute in boiling water. Plunge into cold water, drain well, and add to stew. Stir well to heat through and serve.

SERVES 6

PORK

CAROLINE'S HAM HOCKS AND BEANS

My three favorite dishes all happen to be the culinary creations of my own household, which is, of course, gastronomically incestuous. Here's the recipe for Caroline Murphy's ham hocks and lima beans, which I could kill for. (*PLN*)

> 4 smoked ham hocks
> Water to cover ham hocks
> 4 10-ounce boxes frozen lima beans
> Black pepper

Cook the ham hocks in water to cover until almost tender. Add lima beans and pepper to taste. Cook until beans are tender.

The only problem with this dish is that the ham hocks must be of top quality with lots of meat on them, and good ham hocks are hard to find. But if you tell your butcher in advance, he can usually turn up some good ones for you.

SERVES 4

Step one in the
evolution of
Newman's Creamed
Spinach (see page 84
for recipe).

An old Newman ritual:
creaming the spinach.

Newman's law: always season poultry
before cooking.

There's always a "dill"
moment when
Newman's in the
kitchen.

Another Newman law:
put enough good wine
in the fish sauce and
your guests will never
complain about the
taste.

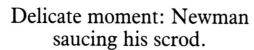

Delicate moment: Newman
saucing his scrod.

PLN with his
famous Dilled Filets
of Scrod à la
Newman (see page
40 for recipe) before
surrendering it to
the oven.

PLN after rescuing his
famous Scrod à la
Newman from the oven.

If you want to hear
Newman purr, give
him sliced tomatoes,
diced Bermuda
onions, and a liberal
dollop of his salad
dressing.

Newman and Hotchner in the kitchen,
the logical successors to Laurel and
Hardy.

Newman proving that he can
dish it out as well as he can
take it.

Ursula Hotchner, A. E. Hotchner, and the chef
with his scrod offering.

PORK FILET MADEIRA

1 medium onion, chopped fine
3 tablespoons butter
2½ pounds pork tenderloin,
   cut into 2-inch pieces
1 cup Madeira
1 cup heavy cream
1 6-ounce jar pearl onions
Salt and pepper
Paprika
1 tablespoon dried thyme *or*
   3 tablespoons fresh thyme
½ pound green beans, cooked al dente,
   refreshed in cold water, and drained

Brown onion in butter over medium heat, remove, and set aside. Brown pork well and return onion to pan. Pour Madeira and cream into pan and stir well. Add pearl onions, salt and pepper to taste, paprika, and thyme. Taste carefully to make sure sauce has flavor. Simmer slowly over low heat about 30 minutes until pork is done and sauce is slightly thickened. Add beans and simmer just enough to warm through.

SERVES 4

VEAL

VEAL MARENGO

This is a dish I learned to cook at the Cordon Bleu, and its success depends on generous amounts of fesh herbs. (*UH*)

> 3 pounds veal shoulder, cut into 2-inch cubes
> 3 tablespoons butter
> 2 tablespoons flour
> 1½ cups white wine
> 1 cup beef bouillon
> Salt and pepper
> 1 tablespoon tomato paste
> 2 tablespoons chopped shallots
> Bouquet garni (bay leaf, parsley, celery leaves,
>   and thyme tied in cheesecloth bag)
> 1 clove garlic, mashed
> 8 ounces mushrooms, sautéed in a little butter
> 2 tomatoes, peeled and sliced, for garnish

Brown veal in butter over high heat. Add flour, stir well, and cook for 2–3 minutes. Add wine, bouillon, salt and pepper to taste, tomato paste, shallots, bouquet garni, and garlic. Simmer covered for 1½ hours over low heat.

Stir in sautéed mushrooms. Add tomatoes, allow to heat for 2–3 minutes without stirring, and serve.

SERVES 6

NEWMAN'S PRAYER

"And he asked
himself –
Good Lord, what have
we unleashed?"

Above the door to
P. L. Newman's office

VEGETABLES

MOSTLY MEATLESS
MAIN DISHES

The dishes I concoct – in my sleep, at the racetrack, and elsewhere – usually incorporate meat, but Joanne and Nell prefer meals that use vegetables, whole grains, and natural foods. So dinner at our house is as likely to feature brown rice or tofu as beef.

While the following recipes can be served as side dishes in smaller, portions, they're hearty enough to serve as entrées. Just toss a salad, slice some homemade bread, and serve. (*PLN*)

THE WOODWARD VEGGYBURGER

What do you do when your husband is a hamburger devotee and you are inclined toward vegetarianism? Well, if you're Joanne Woodward, you invent the Veggyburger, which looks like the Newmanburger but contains no meat and can nestle in a bun just as appealingly as one of my ground chuck specials. (*PLN*)

1 cup chopped onions
2 tablespoons minced garlic
2 tablespoons oil
1 teaspoon dried basil *or*
   2 teaspoons fresh basil
2 cups cooked brown rice
⅔ cup sunflower seeds

⅔ cup cashews
⅓ cup sesame seeds
⅓ cup raw almonds
⅓ cup tamari
   (concentrated soy sauce)
⅔ cup tahini (sesame seed paste)
1 teaspoon oil

Sauté onions and garlic in 2 tablespoons oil. When onions are translucent, add basil and mix well.

Add mixture to rice. Grind in blender all of the seeds and nuts until fine. Add to rice along with tamari and tahini. Shape into patties and brown in nonstick pan in 1 teaspoon oil.

Veggyburgers should be served in pita bread or burger buns with the usual anointments (ketchup, mustard, relish, etc.).

SERVES 6–8

BAKED VEGETABLES

This variation on the Veggyburger is provided by Wilma Kail, Joanne's good friend, who shares Joanne's antipathy toward meat.

    3 potatoes, peeled and sliced thin
    2 long, thin eggplants (Japanese are perfect),
       cut crosswise into 1½-inch slices
    1 green pepper, seeded and cut into strips.
    1 red pepper, seeded and cut into strips
    1 large onion, halved and sliced
    2 small or 1 large zucchini, cut into ½-inch slices
    1 large tomato, cut into chunks
    1 head garlic, separated into cloves, unpeeled
    1 tablespoon dried oregano
    Pepper
    1 tablespoon olive oil

Lightly oil large baking dish. Arrange sliced potatoes on bottom and around sides of baking dish. Arrange other vegetables in alternating pattern on top of potatoes and scatter tomato chunks and garlic cloves over all. Season with oregano and pepper to taste.

Cover pan with foil and bake in preheated 375°F oven until bubbling, about 45 minutes. Uncover and bake 10–15 minutes longer or until all vegetables are tender.

SERVES 6–8

MEXICAN BEAN PIE

2 cups masa harina (Mexican cornmeal;
   do not substitute regular cornmeal)
Salt
1½–2 cups water
2 8- to 10-ounce cans pinto beans
16–20 ounces spaghetti sauce
1 teaspoon each ground cumin and ground coriander
1 small bottle (7 ounces) red salsa
   (Mexican hot sauce) *or* to taste
1 medium onion, chopped
12–16 ounces Monterey Jack cheese

Mix masa harina, 2 pinches salt, and 1½–2 cups water. Knead like dough for 5 minutes until mixed. Form into 8–12 balls and roll into circles on unfloured surface or between 2 sheets of wax paper. They should be ⅛–1⁄16 inch thick. (Rolling them out between sheets of wax paper makes it easier to pick them up.) Fry each tortilla in a lightly greased frying pan over medium heat for 3–5 minutes on each side. Keep warm in damp towels.

While making tortillas, heat beans separately over low heat with the spaghetti sauce. Add cumin, coriander, and salsa to taste. Add onion to spaghetti sauce mixture.

When tortillas are cooked, place one layer in a 10″ x 10″ x 4″ heatproof dish. Coat with a ½-inch layer of beans, a layer of spaghetti sauce, a layer of grated cheese, a layer of tortillas, and so on, ending with cheese. Bake in preheated 350°F oven for 45 minutes to 1 hour until lightly browned on top.

Note: You can substitute 12 small or 8 large fresh store-bought corn tortillas.

VEGETABLE POT PIE

By slightly reducing the amount of vegetables and substituting chicken and chicken stock, you can also make a fantastic chicken pot pie with this recipe. (*NN*)

1 cup peeled and cubed potatoes
4 teaspoons butter
4 tablespoons whole wheat *or* white flour
1½ cups water
2 teaspoons soy sauce
1–2 tablespoons Vogue vegetable stock *or* 1–2 tablespoons powdered chicken broth (available at health food stores)
1 tablespoon nutritional yeast flakes (available at health food stores; also known as edible yeast or brewer's yeast)

Pepper
½ cup cubed carrots
1 medium onion, chopped (about ½ cup)
1 cup broccoli flowerets
¼ cup corn niblets
¼ cup peas
Dough for two-crust 9-inch pie (whole wheat pastry is best, but you can substitute store-bought crust)

Parboil potatoes for 10 minutes over medium heat. Drain. Melt butter in pan over low heat and stir in flour until very thick. Thin with 1½ cups water, adding slowly and stirring constantly. To this add soy sauce, Vogue vegetable stock to taste, nutritional yeast flakes, and pepper to taste, stirring constantly.

Roll out bottom crust and fit into 9″ pie plate. Place vegetables in pie crust and cover with sauce. Put top crust on pie, crimp edges, and make a couple of slits in crust as steam vents. Bake in preheated 350°F oven until lightly browned, 45 minutes to 1 hour.

SERVES 4–6

MARINATED GINGER TOFU OVER CRISPY BROWNED SOBA NOODLES

I used to buy tofu occasionally and attempts to scramble it, eat raw, etc., only to be disgusted by its lack of flavor. Finally, I discovered that the trick to using tofu is that it is mainly a carrier for flavors. It is very rich in protein and contains no cholesterol. If you are willing to experiment, you can make anything from main courses to desserts with it.

For this dinner recipe you can use just about any vegetable you want, particularly Chinese vegetables such as bok choy, which require less cooking time than many Western vegetables. Delicate vegetables such as bok choy and red peppers should not be simmered with the tofu, but placed in the marinade before putting the dish in the oven.

Even if you have never tried tofu and are generally skeptical about new foods, I promise you will enjoy this dish. (*NN*)

1 pound tofu
⅔ cup tamari or regular soy sauce
2¼ cups water
2 teaspoons grated fresh
   gingerroot
1 large onion, chopped coarse
½ large red pepper, chopped
   coarse

2 stalks celery,
   sliced ¼–½ inch thick
3 stalks bok choy
1 large zucchini, sliced
   ½ inch thick
2⅓ cups water
8 ounces soba noodles
   (available in Oriental markets)
3 tablespoons sesame oil

Simmer tofu in soy sauce with water, ginger, and onion

for 1 hour. Allow marinade to sit for at least 1 hour or up to 5. Place all vegetables in a large, shallow, ovenproof dish and pour tofu and marinade over them. Cook in preheated 350°F oven for 30–60 minutes depending on how you like your tofu or how much time you have. I usually cook it until the tofu is browned and the sauce is bubbly.

While the tofu is cooking, place the soba noodles in boiling water with 1 tablespoon sesame oil and cook al dente. Drain and place in nonstick pan over medium-high along with remaining 2 tablespoons sesame oil. Spread noodles so they cover pan evenly and cook until darkly browned or lightly burned. To serve, spoon tofu mixture over individual portions of fried noodles. *Voilà!*

SERVES 4

LAYERED CHEESE SOUFFLÉ

Marcia Franklin

Marcia Franklin has been the majordomo of my private office for many years. She takes care of my film life, my racing life, my social appointments, and my Newman's Own life. That does not leave much time for Marcia to dabble in her kitchen, but she has enough time to produce a few delectables, a sample of which is offered here. (*PLN*)

6 eggs, lightly beaten
½ teaspoon dry mustard
½ teaspoon salt
Dash pepper
Dash Tabasco sauce

2 cups milk
6 slices buttered bread, crusts
    removed, cut into cubes
1 10-ounce package sharp
    cheddar cheese, grated

Beat eggs until frothy. Add seasoning and milk. Alternate layers of bread and cheese in a 10″ × 13″ casserole. Pour egg mixture over bread and cheese, cover, and refrigerate overnight. The next day, let stand at room temperature and bake for 1 hour at 250°F.

SERVES 8

ZUCCHINI CRUST PIZZA

3½ cups coarsely grated zucchini
Salt
⅓ cup flour
3 eggs, lightly beaten
⅔ cup grated Parmesan cheese
2-3 tablespoons olive oil
1½ cups or more grated mozzarella cheese
2 tablespoons minced fresh basil *or* 1 teaspoon
   dried basil
Salt and pepper
Spaghetti sauce
Pizza toppings as desired: peppers, onions, mushrooms,
   anchovies, etc.

Place zucchini in bowl and salt lightly. Let sit for 15 minutes, then squeeze small handfuls as hard as possible to remove water. Roll in towel and twist to release more water. Mix zucchini, flour, eggs, Parmesan, about 2 tablespoons oil, ½ cup mozzarella, basil, and salt and pepper to taste. Spread on very well-oiled baking pan, cookie sheet, or pizza pan. Place in preheated 350°F oven and cook until top is dry and browned, 20–25 minutes. Brush a little oil on surface and broil for a few minutes, taking care not to burn. Spread on a layer of spaghetti sauce, 1 cup or more mozzarella, and any toppings. Return pizza to oven and bake at 350°F until browned, about 25 minutes.

SERVES 4

PROSCIUTTO ROLLS (INVOLTINI DI PROSCIUTTO)

Giovanna Folonari, Director,
Ruffino Tuscan Experience (Florence, Italy)

Who else but Giovanna Folonari, one of Italy's leading hostesses and director of her own cooking school, would have the courage to serve Newman's Own spaghetti sauce in Italy, delighting not only her guests but also some of Italy's leading chefs!

3 medium-size eggplants
Salt
½ pound mozzarella cheese
Flour
Extra-virgin olive oil for frying
⅔ pound prosciutto

1–2 tablespoons butter
3 tablespoons or more
  Newman's Own spaghetti sauce
  or homemade spaghetti sauce
⅓ cup grated Parmesan cheese

Wash and dry the eggplant. Slice very thin crosswise. Place in layers on a chopping board and sprinkle with salt. Tilt the board and leave for 1 hour until the eggplant eliminates its bitter liquid. Meanwhile, cut the mozzarella into cubes.

When the hour is up, dry the eggplant and flour the slices. Fry in hot oil and drain on paper towels.

Cut the prosciutto into thin slices the same size as the eggplant slices. On each slice of eggplant, place a slice of prosciutto and a few cubes of the mozzarella. Roll up the eggplant and seal with a toothpick.

Butter a baking dish and place the eggplant rolls in it. Add spaghetti sauce, sprinkle with the grated Parmesan, and dot with remaining butter.

Bake in preheated 200°F oven for 15 minutes.

SERVES 8

VEGETABLE AND RICE SIDE DISHES

RÖSTI

4–6 medium potatoes, peeled and grated
1 medium onion, chopped fine
Salt and pepper
3 tablespoons cooking oil

To grate potatoes, use a hand grater or the grating blade of a food processor, pressing firmly with the pusher so that the potatoes are julienne. Mix with onion and salt and pepper to taste. Cover the bottom of a 10″ skillet with half the oil and add potatoes, pressing them into a pancake shape about ¾-inch thick. Cover and adjust heat so that the potatoes become brown and crispy in about 8–10 minutes. Carefully invert potato pancake onto lid, add more oil to skillet, and slide pancake back into pan and cook until brown on the other side, about 8 minutes. It should be crisp.

Note: Chopped bacon can be added with onions for an additional flavor treat.

SERVES 4

82

RISOTTO ALLA MILANESE

Sylvia Wachtel

The last time Joanne and Paul came to our house for dinner, I served this risotto with osso buco and a Barolo red wine. We felt *molto Italiano*!

> ½ cup (1 stick) butter
> 1 large onion, chopped or sliced
> 1½ cups rice
> 1 wineglass dry white wine (about 6 ounces)
> 8 cups hot water
> 2 chicken bouillon cubes
> 1 teaspoon salt
> Pinch saffron
> Grated Parmesan cheese

Melt butter in heavy saucepan over low heat. Add onion and cook until tender. Pour rice into saucepan, stirring just enough to prevent sticking to bottom of pan. Add wine. When rice has absorbed the wine, add hot water a little at a time, the chicken bouillon cubes, and salt. Raise heat. When rice has cooked for about 10 minutes (cook for 5 additional minutes if softer rice is desired) gradually adding up to ¼ cup additional hot water if necessary for softer rice. Remove from heat, add Parmesan cheese to taste, and serve immediately.

SERVES 6

NEWMAN'S CREAMED SPINACH

1 pound fresh spinach
⅛ teaspoon ground nutmeg
1 3–ounce package cream cheese, softened
½ cup heavy cream
1 egg

Wash spinach and trim ends. Place spinach in saucepan with just water that clings to leaves. Sprinkle with nutmeg. Cover and steam 2–3 minutes or just until leaves are wilted. Drain any excess liquid. Finely chop spinach and return to saucepan.

Beat cream cheese in small bowl until fluffy. Gradually beat in heavy cream and egg until well blended. Stir cream cheese mixture into chopped spinach. Heat over medium heat, stirring frequently until well blended and creamy. Serve immediately.

SERVES 4

LOQUESTO'S RATATOUILLE

⅓ cup oil (approximately)
3 cloves garlic, crushed
1 large onion, chopped
1 eggplant (about 1¼ pounds)
½ cup flour
2 yellow squash (about ½ pound)
4 small zucchini (about 1 pound)
2 medium green peppers
1 32-ounce jar Newman's Own spaghetti sauce with mushrooms *or*
    1 quart of your favorite homemade spaghetti sauce with
    sautéed mushrooms added to taste
1 cup white wine
½ cup stuffed green olives, sliced

Heat oil and sauté garlic and onion in it until glazed. Cut stem from eggplant and cut eggplant into 1-inch cubes or wedges. Toss with flour and add to pan. Sauté 10 minutes. Trim stems from squash and zucchini and cut into ½-inch wedges about 1½ inches long. Add to pan and cook 10 minutes. Cut green peppers into strips, add to pan, toss lightly, and cook 10 minutes. Add spaghetti sauce with mushrooms and white wine and cook about 20 minutes, until vegetables are tender and sauce is slightly reduced. Add sliced olives. Serve hot or at room temperature. Keeps well in refrigerator.

SERVES 10–12

85

NEWMAN'S LAW

*"If we ever have a plan,
we're screwed!"*

P. L. Newman to himself at
the Stork Club urinal, 1983

BREADS
AND CEREALS

WHOLE WHEAT RAISIN SCONES

While in England this spring, I managed to get a recipe for this traditional teatime treat from a family friend. Her scones were made with white flour and sugar, which I have changed to whole wheat and honey as a matter of personal preference. They can be made either way or somewhere in between; white flour makes lighter scones. Best served at teatime with heavy doses of butter and jam. (*NN*)

½ cup (1 stick) butter
¼ cup honey
2 cups whole wheat flour

⅓ cup milk
3 teaspoons baking soda
¼ cup raisins

Combine butter, honey, and flour with your hands until it resembles coarse meal. Stir in milk, baking soda, and raisins, making sure all ingredients are well mixed until they form a doughy ball. Lightly flour the rolling surface and the top of the dough ball. Roll dough evenly in all directions until ¾–1 inch thick. Using the rim of a glass or a cookie cutter with a diameter of 2–2½ inches, make individual scones and place on a well-greased and floured cookie sheet. Cook in preheated 350°F oven for 20–30 minutes or until browned on top. Can be served hot out of the oven or cold.

SESAME LOAVES

My family is quite fond of this wonderful bread recipe. Consequently, it doesn't last long in our household, especially since it goes so well with soups, salads, or sandwiches such as Caroline Murphy's Tuna Salad (see page 36 for recipe). I would love to lie and say it is my original creation, but I must give credit where credit is due. This recipe was given to me by my family friend and a professional cook, Cary Bell of Bar Harbor, Maine. (*NN*)

1 cup boiling water	1 teaspoon sugar or honey
1 cup quick-cooking oats	3½ cups whole wheat flour
1 cup unhulled sesame seeds	1 teaspoon salt
1½ cups warm water	1 handful cornmeal
1 teaspoon dry yeast	

Mix boiling water, oats, and sesame seeds together and allow to cool. In a large bowl, combine warm water, yeast, and sugar and put in a warm place. When the yeast mixture is bubbly (5–15 minutes), add flour, salt, and sesame mixture until dough forms a ball. (This may require a bit more flour.) Flour the surface on which you will be kneading your dough (something smooth usually works best), as well as your hands and the dough itself. Then transfer dough to the floured surface and knead well for 10–15 minutes. Allow to rise for 45 minutes and then knead again. Shape into 2 long loaves and place on a greased, cornmeal-covered pan. Bake in a preheated 350°F oven about 30–50 minutes, until golden brown and hollow-sounding when tapped with a wooden spoon or fingers.

MAKES 2 LOAVES

ZUCCHINI BREAD

Joanne Woodward

3 cups flour
1 teaspoon baking soda
1 teaspoon baking powder
1 teaspoon ground cinnamon
1 teaspoon salt

3 eggs
1 cup sugar
1 cup oil
1 teaspoon vanilla
2 cups grated zucchini

Sift flour, baking soda, baking powder, cinnamon, and salt together. Beat eggs until foamy. Add sugar, oil, vanilla, and sifted dry ingredients a little at a time. The mixture will be thick. Add the zucchini; the mixture will be gummy. Pour into 2 well-greased 8½″ × 4½″ × 2½″ loaf pans and bake at 350°F for 1 hour. Check at 50 minutes; if a toothpick comes out clean, bread is done. Great served hot or cold. May be frozen.

MAKES 2 LOAVES

CARROT BREAD

Sylvia Wachtel

This is my mother's wonderful recipe. She wouldn't dare come for a visit without bringing along extra loaves for Joanne and Paul.

1 pound carrots (approximately)
1 6-ounce can crushed pineapple, drained
2 ounces crystallized ginger, diced
2 tablespoons lemon juice
2 cups sugar
1 cup plus 2 tablespoons oil (approximately)
3 eggs, lightly beaten
3 tablespoons grated orange peel

3 cups flour
2 teaspoons baking soda
2 teaspoons baking powder
½ teaspoon salt
2 teaspoons ground cinnamon
½ teaspoon freshly grated nutmeg
½ teaspoon ground allspice
1 teaspoon vanilla extract
1 cup regular (noninstant) oats
½ cup chopped pecans

Peel and grate carrots to produce roughly 1½ cups finely grated carrots and 1½ cups more coarsely grated carrots.

Combine carrots, pineapple, ginger, and lemon juice in a bowl and let rest while you beat together sugar and oil until creamy. To the oil-sugar mixture, add the 3 eggs and the grated orange peel.

Combine carrot mixture with orange peel mixture. Mix well.

Sift together flour, baking soda, baking powder, salt, cinnamon, nutmeg, and allspice. To this mixture, add vanilla.

Beat carrot mixture with flour mixture. To this, add oats and pecans. Stir until well mixed and spoon into 2 8½″ × 4½″ × 2½″ oiled loaf pans. Bake in preheated 350°F oven for 45–55 minutes. The loaves are done when a testing needle comes away clean. Cool in pans on racks.

MAKES 2 LOAVES

JOANNE'S CEREAL

Joanne's culinary repertoire is limited, but she makes up in quality what she lacks in quantity. Her breakfast cereal is the best way for anyone to start the day, and it would certainly become a Newman's Own product if it weren't for the complicated process required to create it. It is best to make a large batch of the cereal, which can then be kept in the refrigerator for several weeks. (*PLN*)

1¼ cups oil
1½ cups water
2 pounds honey
1 pound oats
2 pounds almonds

1 pound sunflower seeds
½ cup sesame seeds
1 cup chopped cashews
1 cup chopped walnuts
4 cups wheat germ, roasted

Mix oil, water, and honey together. Mix dry ingredients together. Combine all. Spread thinly on cookie sheets. Bake in 325°F oven and keep turning until golden brown (about 20–30 minutes). Cool and keep in tins.

NEWMAN'S LAW

"If I want to test a new restaurant, I order something I don't like and dare them to make me like it."

P. L. Newman

DESSERTS AND SNACKS

WHIPPED CREAM-FILLED BANANA CAKE

1½ cups sugar
8 tablespoons (1 stick) butter
4 bananas, mashed
4 eggs
4 teaspoons baking soda
4 tablespoons boiling milk

2 cups flour
2 pints cold heavy cream
Sugar
Cocoa
Powdered sugar (optional)

Cream sugar and butter together. Add mashed bananas and eggs and mix well.

Dissolve baking soda in boiling milk. Add to butter and egg mixture, along with the flour.

Pour batter into 2 8½″ cake pans and bake in preheated 350°F oven 20–30 minutes until browned and the center springs back when touched.

Whip cream until peaks form, adding sugar and cocoa to taste. You can either frost the whole cake or put all the whipped cream in the middle and sprinkle powdered sugar on the top.

SERVES 10–12

EGGLESS, BUTTERLESS, WONDERFUL SPICY RAISIN WALNUT CAKE

When I first experimented with this recipe I was surprised by how good it was without any eggs or butter. However, the nuts contain oil, and that makes up for any lack of butter. (*NN*)

1 cup brown sugar
½ cup molasses
¾ cup milk
¼ cup very strong coffee
4 teaspoons baking powder
1 teaspoon ground cinnamon
½ teaspoon each: nutmeg, clove, allspice, mace
2 cups whole wheat flour
½ teaspoon salt
1 pound raisins
2 cups walnuts

Combine sugar, molasses, milk, and coffee. Sift dry ingredients together, saving ¼ cup flour. Dredge raisins in ¼ cup flour. Mix dry ingredients with liquid ingredients and add raisins and walnuts. Pour into well-buttered 8½″ × 4½″ × 2½″ loaf pan and bake in preheated 350°F oven for 45 minutes to 1 hour or until top is browned and toothpick inserted in center comes out clean.

MAKES 1 LOAF CAKE

PINEAPPLE AND PEAR UPSIDE-DOWN CAKE

8 tablespoons (1 stick) butter or margarine
¾ cup plus 4 tablespoons honey
1 egg
¾ cup whole wheat flour
¾ cup white flour
½ teaspoon salt
1¼ teaspoons baking powder
⅓ cup milk
2 teaspoons vanilla
2 tablespoons raspberry liqueur
2 or 3 slices pineapple, cut into small wedges
1 Bosc pear, cut vertically into wedges

Blend 6 tablespoons of the butter with ¾ cup of the honey, add egg, and mix well.

Sift dry ingredients and add half to butter mixture, then all the milk, and then the rest of the dry ingredients. Add the vanilla until well blended.

Place remaining butter in 9″ round cake pan and melt over low heat. Add raspberry liqueur and remaining honey to butter and stir for 4–5 minutes, until combined. Remove from heat and arrange the fruit decoratively in pan.

Lightly grease the sides of the cake pan and gently spoon in the batter. Cook in preheated 350°F oven for 35–45 minutes or until top is browned and toothpick inserted in center comes out clean. Cool 5–10 minutes before inverting onto plate.

MAKES 1 CAKE

A VARIATION ON
THE THEME OF PASHKA

Ina Balin

(Ina Balin first met the Newmans when they were in *From the Terrace* together, and over the years they have remained friends.)

I was living in Spain in 1966 and visiting some friends in Barcelona. They brought me along to a dinner party. The food was delicious, topped off by a dessert that was incredible. I asked the hostess for the recipe and she very generously gave it to me saying, "Isn't it amusing that you have to come all the way to Spain to have dinner in a Polish household and take home a Russian recipe?"

Since then, I have kept that recipe in my passport folder and it goes where I go. It went to California when I was there on a visit, and I gave a dinner party that Paul and Joanne attended. Almost everyone there had second helpings, including Paul, who said, "I hardly ever eat any dessert, let alone seconds."

Because this dish is very rich, it is best to serve small portions, so your guests won't feel so guilty when they ask for seconds. This dessert also makes a beautiful centerpiece on your table. Enjoy!

4 8-ounce packages cream cheese
1 cup (2 sticks) butter
3 egg yolks
2 cups sifted powdered sugar

2 teaspoons vanilla
1 cup toasted slivered almonds
2–3 pints fresh or frozen
   strawberries

Let cream cheese, butter, and egg yolks stand at room temperature at least 2 hours.

Beat cheese in mixing bowl with a wooden spoon or blend at low speed in electric mixer. Add butter and continue beating. When well blended, add sugar, then yolks, one at a time. Add vanilla and fold in almonds.

Wash and dry inside of a Pashka mold or a new 2-quart clay or plastic flowerpot with drain holes in the bottom. Line the pot with a double thickness of cheese-cloth wrung out in cold water. Spoon cheese mixture into the pot to the brim. Cover with plastic wrap and refrigerate several hours or overnight on a plate.

To unmold, trim around and discard top of the cheesecloth. Invert a dessert plate over the opening of the flowerpot and quickly turn the whole thing upside down. Place on table and gently lift off pot, tugging at the cheesecloth lining if necessary. When the pot is clear, gently remove the cheesecloth.

Garnish the base and top of the Pashka with whole strawberries and strawberry halves. Serve with additional crushed, sweetened strawberries as a sauce. You may add some brandy or liqueur to the sauce if you wish.

SERVES 16–18

WONDERFUL SESAME PEANUT BUTTER CANDY TREATS

1½ cups unhulled sesame seeds
1⅔ cups barley malt (available in health food stores)
⅓ cup smooth or chunky peanut butter
½ cup raisins

Toast sesame seeds over low heat until they are lightly toasted. They will be slightly browned and have a different taste from untoasted seeds.

When cool, add barley malt, peanut butter, and raisins. Combine very well. This is best done with your hands, which should be greased with oil first. Scrape hands with a butter knife and use a coffee scooper to make individual treats. Wrap each in tin foil or wax paper. They last for weeks!

MAKES ABOUT 28 TREATS

PROFITEROLES

If you've never been applauded at the end of a meal, try serving this dessert. It's guaranteed to earn you a standing ovation. It has never failed me, and invariably guests who rarely eat desserts ask for seconds. (*UH*)

1 cup water
8 tablespoons (1 stick) butter
¼ teaspoon salt
1 cup sifted all-purpose flour

4 eggs
Ice cream *or* whipped cream
Hot Fudge Sauce (see following recipe)

In a saucepan, combine water, butter, and salt. Bring to brisk boil. Remove from heat and add the flour all at once. Stir vigorously until mixture leaves the sides of the pan and forms a ball around the spoon. Add eggs, one by one, beating until mixture is smooth and glossy after each addition. Drop the mixture by rounded teaspoonfuls (or use pastry bag) onto a greased baking sheet, about 2 inches apart. Bake at 450°F for about 10 minutes, reduce heat to 350°F, and bake until rigid and there are no bubbles of fat on surface, about 15–20 minutes more. Five minutes before they are done, pierce each puff with a sharp knife to allow steam to escape. Remove from oven and cool.

Just before serving, cut off the tops, fill with ice cream or whipped cream, replace the tops, and cover with Hot Fudge Sauce.

MAKES ABOUT 24 SMALL PUFFS

HOT FUDGE SAUCE

5 squares semi-sweet chocolate
1½ tablespoons unsalted butter
2 tablespoons sugar

½ cup milk
2 tablespoons heavy cream

Melt chocolate with butter and sugar in the milk and heavy cream over medium heat. Bring to a boil and simmer, stirring constantly, 1–2 minutes. Pour into a serving bowl and cool.

MAKES 1 CUP

MOLASSES BALLS

1½ cups light molasses
¼ cup (½ stick) salted butter
2 cups raisins

1 cup toasted unsalted
   sunflower seeds
6 cups popped popcorn

Heat molasses over medium heat and mix butter in well. Add raisins and sunflower seeds until evenly distributed. Drizzle mixture over popcorn, mixing well until thoroughly coated. Lightly grease hands and shape into balls. Wrap in wax paper and refrigerate to store.

MAKES 6–8 BALLS

COFFEE BAVARIAN

1 envelope unflavored gelatin
¼ cup cold water
3 eggs, separated
⅔ cup sugar
⅔ cup milk, scalded
1 teaspoon vanilla
½ cup very strong black coffee
1 cup cold heavy cream

Soften gelatin in cold water and set aside. In top of double boiler set over hot water, beat egg yolks and sugar until light-colored. Gradually add the hot milk, stirring constantly. Cook over hot water until slightly thickened. Add gelatin, vanilla, and coffee, stirring until gelatin is completely dissolved. Chill until it becomes very syrupy. Beat the heavy cream until stiff and fold into the coffee mixture. Beat whites until stiff but not dry and fold in gently but thoroughly. Pour into a 1-quart mold that has been rinsed in cold water and refrigerate at least 6 hours.

SERVES 6

POPCANDY

1⅔ cups maple syrup
½ cup (1 stick) butter
½ tablespoon ground nutmeg

Mixed together:
7 cups popped popcorn
1 cup chopped toasted almonds
1 cup chopped pecans

In a heavy saucepan, combine maple syrup, butter, and nutmeg, boiling until mixture reaches 270°F on a candy thermometer (the soft crack stage), stirring occasionally. Dribble onto popcorn and nut mixture until well covered. May be made into bite-size popcorn balls and wrapped in wax paper or pressed into a large well-oiled pan and broken up into smaller pieces when hardened. Keep in a container with a tight lid.

MAKES 7–9 BALLS

PEANUT BUTTER POPCORN

2 cups smooth or crunchy peanut butter
2 tablespoons honey

6 cups popped popcorn
3 cups dry-roasted peanuts, chopped medium-fine

Place peanut butter in saucepan over low heat and mix in honey. When well mixed, drizzle over popcorn and mix well. Mixture should be sticky. Place chopped peanuts on a large flat pan or plate. Oil hands lightly to prevent sticking and shape popcorn into balls. Roll popcorn balls in peanuts and wrap in wax paper. Refrigerate to store.

MAKES 6–8 BALLS

PART III

THE UNTOLD TALE OF NEWMAN'S OWN

In the beginning, there were two friends,
adrift in a sea of poor tastes.

HOW P. L. NEWMAN AND A. E. HOTCHNER BECAME FOOD TYCOONS

A Diversion by A. E. Hotchner

You are probably wondering how it happened that P. L. Newman, who is rather steadily employed in his chosen profession, and I, who am somewhat sporadically employed in mine, wound up in the food business. For as long as I can remember, Newman has been rejecting so-called house dressings and concocting his own mix. Captains, maître d's, and sometimes the restaurant owners themselves scurried around to assemble Newman's ingredients. When we first ate at Elaine's, one of New York's "in" restaurants, virtually all the waiters and Elaine herself gathered round as Paul blended and tasted the ingredients that had been brought to him from the kitchen.

I have watched this scene repeated in a Greek diner, at a wedding party, and in various restaurants from coast to coast. When his kids went off to school, they would ask him to fill a couple of empty wine bottles with the salad dressing for them to take along.

All well and good until that day, a few years back, when Paul came over one afternoon to watch a football game and said, "I've got a neat idea for Christmas presents—I'm going to give all my friends bottles of my salad dressing. They're always asking me for the recipe, so I'll fill up all the empty wine bottles I've been saving and play Santa Claus. Good idea, huh?'

Meeting the challenge.

"Great – they'll love it," I said naïvely.

"When can we start?"

"Start what?"

"Making the dressing. I figure you and I can do it in an afternoon. How about tomorrow?"

As devious as Tom Saywer, he is. It took us eight hours of steady labor to mix it, bottle it, cork it, and wrap it. But Newman's friends were delighted, and it was a ritual Paul and I followed every Christmas after that, each year taking longer than the year before as the list of requests for "Newman's Own salad dressing" grew longer and longer.

But finally my sagging back cracked under the mounting pressure. It was the year that it took us three days of sweatshop labor down in Newman's cellar to turn out enough bottles to satisfy his list, by then three pages long. And at the end of the third day, Paul stood in the center of the cellar, surrounded by all those filled bottles, and suggested that we do another hundred bottles and put them up for sale in local food stores.

"You can't stand the thought that on Christmas Day there will be

Moment of creation.

people around here eating salad without your dressing on it, that it?'

He nodded. "How can we be so selfish? Spread good cheer, I say. What's a couple more days of bottling?"

I didn't tell him. Instead I said, "It's against the law."

"What is? There is absolutely nothing in my dressing that's illegal."

"The Pure Food Law. You have to have certain certificates."

"OK, let's look into it."

That was how it started, innocently enough, but over the next several months Newman was driven by his desire to market his dressing. Scarcely a day passed without Paul's calling from some unlikely place to discuss a newly discovered source for the perfect olive oil, the perfect red wine vinegar, or the perfect mustard that he constantly sought. He phoned me from racetracks in between races, from mobile dressing rooms while shooting *Absence of Malice* and *The Verdict*, and from airports on his way to make speeches ond behalf of the nuclear freeze movement.

That's when I said, "Listen, Paul, we've been friends for twenty-odd

Mixing it up for friends and neighbors.

Joy to the world—spirit of giving.

Begging for more but the cupboard is bare.

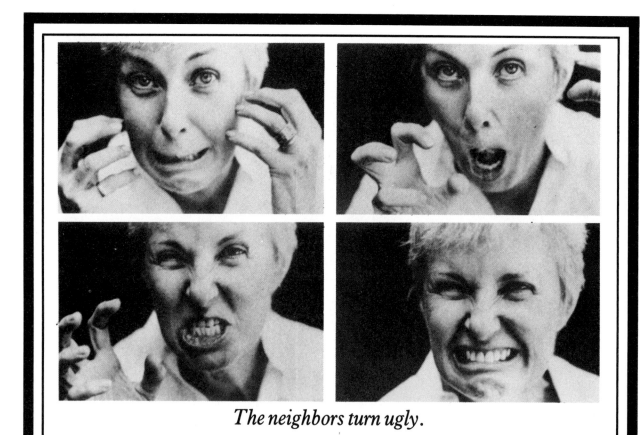

The neighbors turn ugly.

Snookered!

All winter long—hostage in a sweatshop.

years [some of them *really* odd!], and I wonder why you're so fixed on marketing your dressing. I ask you, would Clark Gable sell salad dressing? Would Tyrone Power? Humphrey Bogart? Isn't it a little tacky?"

"It's all-natural," Newman said, a touch of pique in his tone. "Just look at the labels on all these other dressings – full of gums, preservatives, chemical additives – that's why."

Fed up!

It took us a while, but we finally found just the right olive oil and a soybean oil that mated nicely with it in a 50–50 mix. Our most extensive search was for the red wine vinegar that would satisfy Newman's finicky taste, but that materialized one day when we were having lunch at Mario's little Italian restaurant at the Westport railroad station. Mario himself had come out of the kitchen to watch Paul go through his mixing

112

Sweet smell . . .

of freedom!

routine. One taste of the vinegar on the end of his fork, and Paul exuberantly embraced Mario Italian style.

The search for other ingredients was just as arduous (fresh onion and garlic, spices and herbs), but even after all the components satisfied him, Paul still had to arrive at precisely the right proportions that would produce the taste he was after. Perfectionist that he is, Paul continued experimenting until that fateful day when he came careening up my driveway in his supercharged Volkswagen, waving a bottle of his dressing aloft.

All's well that ends well.

"This is it! This is it!" he shouted, much the same as Bell must have announced his telephone and Edison his electric light bulb.

Well, he was right. We broke open a head of lettuce and sprinkled on the dressing, and our whoops and hollers could be heard for miles around.

114

P. L. NEWMAN ON THE ORIGIN OF HIS SPAGHETTI SAUCE

"Working twelve hour days . . . wrecked . . . hungry . . . arrive home, deserted by wife and children . . . cursing! Scan the cupboard – one package spaghetti, one bottle marinara sauce. Run to kitchen, cook – junk! YUK! Lie down, snooze . . . visions of culinary delights . . . Venetian ancestor tickles my ear, tickle, tickle . . . sauce talk . . . MAMA MIA! Dash to vegetable patch . . . yum-yum . . . boil water . . . activate spaghetti . . . ditto the sauce . . . slurp, slurp . . . Terrifico! Magnifico! Slurp! Carumba! Bottle the sauce! Share with guys on streetcar . . . Ah, me, finally immortal!"

HOTCHNER'S LURID BUT TRUE ACCOUNT OF THE GENESIS OF NEWMAN'S SONGFEST AT HANRATTY'S BAR & GRILL

It was not until we actually began to market Newman's salad dressing that I was able to spend Christmas with my family around the tree, like everyone else. Before that, as I have explained, for four consecutive Christmases I was toiling away in Newman's basement, chained to the furnace, filling an endless collection of empty wine bottles to be given as presents to Newman's friends and neighbors. On Christmas day, reeking of olive oil, vinegar, and mustard, I lay exhausted like a beached whale as my little family bravely carried on their yuletide festivities without me.

But just because I had been sprung from the cellar once we got into the stores did not mean I had been fully liberated. No, as my first unencumbered Christmas approached, Newman called and said, "Let's have a jolly lunch at Mario's Restaurant down at the railroad station." Like a fool, naïvely unsuspecting his Machiavellian intent, I came to the restaurant lightheartedly, with thoughts of minestrone and osso buco dancing in my head. But he did it to me again!

"Hotchner," he said, "we have a crying need, and you're the one to fill it – we need an official salad dressing song."

"Sorry," I said, "I don't deal in salad dressing songs."

"Hotch," he said, with that sincerity I knew only too well from *The Sting*, "we all have to extend ourselves. Let's meet tomorrow same time and see what you've got."

So I burned the midnight oil, and while Sir Arthur Sullivan turned in his grave, I wrote new lyrics to the music he had

116

written for "I Am the Very Model of a Model Major General." The next day Newman read the lyrics, again over pasta at Mario's, and said, "Fine, OK. Who'll we get to sing it?" I knew it was rhetorical and that he already had the answer, so I said nothing. "I've got it," he said. "Pavarotti." So he made a phone call and found out Pavarotti was in a hotel in San Francisco where he was preparing to appear with the San Francisco Opera in *I Pagliacci*.

Either forgetting or not caring that it was three hours earlier in San Francisco, Newman phoned, and a sleepy Italian voice said, "Pronto." After Newman convinced the great Italian tenor that he was really Newman, Pavarotti politely explained that he was sorry but he couldn't sing the salad dressing song because he was rehearsing for the opera. Newman tried to get him to postpone it, but to no avail.

Foolishly thinking we were well out of this potential embarrassment, I started to pocket my ill-conceived song when Newman said, "Not so fast, Hotchner. We *must* have a salad dressing song." It was then that I realized a bigger truth than truth itself: the real reason Newman invented this salad dressing and marketed it goes back to *Butch Cassidy*. The director, George Roy Hill, had promised Newman he could sing "Raindrops Keep Falling on My Head," but it wasn't until the last day of shooting that Newman discovered that George was not going to keep his promise. In an attempt to assuage Newman's disappointment, George offered to let him ride a bicycle, which Newman did, but cycling and singing were not, in Newman's estimation, quid pro quo.

Now, many years later, Newman was finally providing himself with an opportunity to redeem his baritone by inventing a salad dressing, marketing it, and getting a captive press group together to introduce it, thereby providing himself with an occasion when he could SING!

117

NEWMAN'S OWN
SALAD DRESSING SONG

(To the tune of Gilbert and Sullivan's "I Am the Very Model of a Model Major General")

I've tasted all the dressings on the shelves at food emporiums,
And most of them taste like they should be served in vomitoriums.
I'm very well acquainted too with dressings that you mix at home,
And thrust upon the visiting and unsuspecting gastronome.
But as for me I much prefer to eat my salad in the sack,
And that is why in Newman's Own you'll find an aphrodisiac.

Chorus:
And that is why in Newman's Own
*   you'll find an aphrodisiac,*
And that is why in Newman's Own
*   you'll find an aphrodisiac,*
And that is why in Newman's Own
*   you'll find an aphrodisisi – disi – ac.*

Which brings me to the subject of
*   this bottle's true ingredients,*
That I will now reveal to you
*   with candor and expedience.*
In short, when you have tasted
*   it you'll know just what*
*   you're get – ett – ing,*
Feel free to strip and lurch
*   about with naughty pirouet –*
*   ett – ing.*

Chorus:
In short, when you have tasted it
*   you'll know just what you're*
*   get – ett – ing,*
Feel free to strip and lurch about
*   with naughty pirouet – ett – ing.*

118

To find the proper olive oil we searched through several continents,
To find the one that had the most extraordinary redolence,
From sunny Spain to Portugal and then on to Transylvania,
How the hell was I to know we'd find the stuff in Pennsylvania?

And now we had to turn our search a red wine vinegar to find,
And sampling here and sampling there we drunk us got and pretty blind,
The mustard search was just as far until we learned our lesson,
And found exactly what we sought at Hotchner's delicatessen.

Chorus:
And found exactly what we sought at Hotchner's delicatessen,
And found exactly what we sought at Hotchner's delicatessen,
And found exactly what we sought at Hotchner's delica – delica – tess –
    en.

The clever spices we have added are a well-kept mystery,
And everything is natural to ward off flu and dysent'ry!
So now I have explained to you with all my cogent reasonings,
Why I hope that I am known as the man for all good seasonings!

Chorus:
So now he has explained to you with all his cogent reasonings,
Why he hopes that he is known as the man for all good seasonings!

NEWMAN'S SPAGHETTI DUET
WITH JOANNE WOODWARD

Newman's Own Industrial Strength Venetian Spaghetti Sauce was introduced to the world at a gathering at Keen's Chop House in Manhattan. On this occasion, Paul inveigled me to write a spaghetti ballad not only for him, but also for Joanne, who, good sport that she is, gave it the benefit of her reluctant soprano.

(To the tune of Lerner and Loewe's "I've Grown Accustomed to Her Face")

NEWMAN:
I've tasted sauces from the East,
Some made with curdled milk and yeast,
And the spaghetti drenched with grease
That makes you so obese,
It sticks to you,
And tastes like glue,
Those pasta sauces on the shelf,
No self-respecting man would eat.
I have Italian blood that needs a good spaghetti *now and then,*
Malnutrition almost drove me round the bend —
That's when,
There came to me while deep in sleep,
A recipe divine,
A recipe that's mine . . .

(To the tune of Gershwin's "I've Got
Rhythm")

JOANNE:
It's got onions,
It's got garlic,
It's got basil,
Who could ask for anything more?

120

It's got olive
Oil and spices,
It's all nat'ral,
True industrial strength galore!

Pride of Venice,
Rome and Pisa,
It'sa sure that
It'll please ya.

Lots of peppers,
Fresh tomatoes,
Cup of sunshine,
Who could ask for anything more?
Who could ask for anything more?

NEWMAN:
I'm as content as I can be,
That now I have a spaghetti,
Of which my ancestors can be
So justly proud of me –
From Sha – ker Heights,
To Ve – nice nights.
And now Andretti says that he,
Would like to give me the Grand Prix,
For having fin'lly made a sauce that's
*   like he had in Italy,*
He then ran a vic'try lap for him and me,
You see . . .

If you will keep on buying this,
It will become a fact,
Newman won't have to act!

JOANNE AND PAUL:
Who could ask for anything more?
Who could ask for anything more?

121

HIS BARITONE NEWMAN MELLIFLUOUSLY RAISES, TO SING HIS POPCORN'S OLD-FASHIONED PRAISES

Not satisfied with beating up on Gilbert & Sullivan with the salad dressing song in Hollywood (accompanied by the magical ivory tickling of Henry Mancini, shown below), Paul gave the venerable English composers another whack with this popcorn cadenza (God forgive me!), which he warbled when we introduced Newman's Own Oldstyle Picture Show Popcorn at a summer charity fest in Westport, Connecticut.

(To the tune of Gilbert & Sullivan's "I Am the Very Model of a Model Major General")

We gave the world a salad dressing that is truly magnifique,
And then a marinara sauce gourmet Italians call unique,
And now we bring you popcorn with a lot of special properties,
The connoisseurs have all agreed we have produced
*   a crop to please.*
Our popcorn makes you smile when you are suffering
*   dyspepsia,*
And it will goose your appetite when you have anorexia.
And all the horny Englishmen and Finns and
*   Overzealous Czechs,*
Will find that Newman's Own is better
*   than the kinkiest of sex!*

Chorus:
The good news is that Newman's Own
*   is better than the kinkiest of sex,*
The good news is that Newman's Own
*   is better than the kinkiest of sex,*

122

The good news is that Newman's Own
    is better than the kinkiest of sex!

The New York Post *has snooped*
    around to find out our ingredients.
They got it wrong but published it
    with cowardly expedience.
BUT! Our popcorn has integrity
    no one can compromi –ise us,
We wouldn't be surprised if it's
awarded Nobel Pri – izes!

Chorus:
Our popcorn has integrity no one can compromi – ise us,
We wouldn't be surprised if it's awarded Nobel Pri – izes!

To find a popcorn oo-là-là we searched through several continents,
To find the one that had the most extraordinary redolence,
In Turkey, Spain, Iran, Iraq, we searched for popcorn high and low,
How the hell were we to know we'd find it in Ohi – i – o!
It is the color of the sun and pops as white as falling snow,
And if your car should ever stall our hot popcorn will make it go,
The lights are low, your girl says no, and you are really through unless,
You feed her full of Newman's Own and turn her no into a yes!

Chorus:
You feed her full of Newman's Own and turn her no into a yes,
You feed her full of Newman's Own and turn her no into a yes,
You feed her full of Newman's Own and turn her no into a ye – e – es!

Our blend of corn will most assuredly promote good fellow – ship,
And ev'rything is natural to clear up gout and nasal drip!
And now we tell you finally with candor and with clarity,
That you should buy a lot because our profits go to charity!

Chorus:
And now we tell you finally with candor and with clarity,
That you should buy a lot because our profits go to charity!

P. L. Newman and A. E. Hotchner,
doing their best to look philanthropic.

THE PITFALLS AND PRATFALLS OF TWO NEOPHYTE PHILANTHROPISTS

When we began bottling salad dressing in the fall of 1982, it never entered our minds that one day our innocent little venture would make us philanthropists. We just intended to put some bottles of Newman's Own oil and vinegar dressing on the shelves of a few local markets, but within a month there was a groundswell of demand from stores across the country. Within six months we had four factories in operation, our own network of trucks, and Newman's Own had become big business.

It was at the end of our first year of operation, poised by then to introduce a second product – Newman's Own Industrial Strength Spaghetti Sauce – that we set out on the road to philanthropy. We had accumulated $920,000 in profit, more than we ever dreamed we'd be making, and Paul said, "Let's give it all away to them what needs it."

Because we have so little overhead, we are able to generate 16.6 percent pretax profit, six times the food business average of 3.3 percent. What started out as a lark became, to our everlasting amazement, a burgeoning food empire. Not only were our products all over the United States, but we were being widely distributed in such faraway places as Australia, Japan, Canada,

125

Puerto Rico, Guam, and England. In the little over three years we have been in existence, we have sold 18,705,555 bottles of Newman's Own oil and vinegar salad dressing, amounting to $15,525,611 in gross sales, and since Newman's Own Industrial Strength Venetian Spaghetti Sauce has been in existence, the sales figures are 8,371,726 jars, totaling $12,557,589. Our total profit from these two products was approximately four million dollars, every penny of which has been given to deserving charities. Newman's Own Oldstyle Picture Show Popcorn is our newest product which we hope will swell our charity profits even more. In less than a year, we have sold 2,132,493 jars, giving us gross sales of $2,452,367.

It never occurred to us that philanthropists had any trials and tribulations, but now, after three years of dispensing all our profits to deserving recipients, we found that playing Santa Claus often involves making some very tough decisions.

Even though $4 million seems like a lot of money to disburse, it is far short of the needs of all the deserving organizations that petition us, and deciding who and what gets precedence has been a difficult and often heart-touching experience. For every organization that can be helped, there are two other organizations, hurting and needful, that must go begging.

We read all the material that is sent to us by applicants, and then we discuss their merits, but in the final analysis we let our gut feelings make the decisions – gut feelings plus general guidelines we've developed through our experiences over the past few years.

We have no problems with the donations we have made to obvious recipients – Sloan-Kettering Cancer Research, Lahey Clinic, New York Foundling Hospital, Cystic Fibrosis, Society to Advance the Retarded, Jacksonville Wolfson Children's Hospital, Harlem Restoration. We felt, however, that it was also important to make meaningful donations to little-known charities that were in dire need but lacked the publicity to attract donations. For example, this letter which we received from Sister Arlene Welding, School Sister of St. Francis:

Dear Mr. Newman:

This past year I was on the verge of opening a food pantry in the poor section of Hollywood, when the money I had anticipated receiving from United Way and the Catholic Church did not come to be realized. I see far too many people, mostly elderly, eating from garbage cans or containers. So many destitute in this area. I heard over TV this morning that you give away the profit you made in your new business. I was edified to hear this. Would you consider giving some of your profit to help us to open up a food pantry to respond to the needy here in Hollywood? It is dehumanizing for these people to have to resort to asking for food or shelter.

Trusting you will respond to this request in the spirit of compassion and love for the poor, I await your response with concern.

Sincerely yours,
S. Arlene Welding, SSSF

We were pleased to be able to stock Sister Arlene's pantry. We were also gratified to be able to make a contribution to the Burn and Trauma Center for Children that Dr. Wilibald Nagler operates at New York Hospital. We also responded to a touching letter we received from the Princess Yasmin Aga Khan, who is on the Executive Committee of the Alzheimer's Disease Association in Chicago. Although she didn't mention it, Newman and I knew that the princess's mother, Rita Hayworth, is a victim of the disease.

"In the beginning," Paul says, "we were pretty bewildered, trying to decide which among the vast number of deserving charities we should give to. But by now we've got a pretty good philosophy – give to organizations for the very young and the very old. And also, these profits give me a chance to repay those places that helped me when I needed them. Kenyon University, where I went to school, and which whetted my appetite for the stage. Yale University drama school, which firmed my resolve to be an actor. The Neighborhood Playhouse and the Actor's Studio in New York, where marvelous theatre people taught me and encouraged me and put me on the track to a career. It's a kick to be able to give places like these solid grants of money so that they can help other young people as they helped me.

"But the biggest kick Hotch and I get is when we can help little, obscure organizations that cannot attract the attention of big donors. But what is not rewarding is having to turn down all requests from individuals – even the ones that are rather farfetched. Just yesterday, we received a letter from a forty-three-year-old woman who lives with her sixty-four-year-old mother. She informs me that she has found two townhouses in close proximity, for $80,000 each, and if I could see my way clear to send her $160,000 of Newman's Own, Inc., profits, she would be eternally grateful. Although, on the face of it, it sounds like a ludicrous request, the fact is her letter represents a dream that she and her mother have probably shared for years, and it's sad that we can't help her fulfill it."

We have a substantial Canadian Market, and we have transferred our Canadian profits to three charities there: The Hospital for Sick Children, the St. Boniface General Hospital Research Foundation, and the Famous People Players, a remarkable nonprofit group of black light puppeteers who have performed all over the world, most recently in China. Ten of the thirteen members of the troupe are retarded.

As we did with Canada, we also contributed to Australian charities all the profits we realized from the sale of our products there. Ursula Hotchner, who is the international vice president of our company, recently traveled to Melbourne and Sydney to present checks for sizable amounts to the Northcott Crippled Children's School and the Sunshine Helping Hand Association for the Retarded. We will follow this procedure of returning all profits in every foreign country where we do business.

Along with requests we act on, we receive many that do not elicit gut reaction. A man in Arlington, Virginia, would like to open a school to teach judo; a woman in Bloomington, Illinois, maintains a sanctuary for 250 orphaned dogs that are in need of dog food; a Bellevue, Washington, gentleman is corresponding with a Czech widow he would like to marry, but he needs airfare to Czechoslovakia; a woman has designed a calendar featuring adorable kittens but needs $55,000 to put the calendars into production; a group of German war veterans based in Munich writes in German requesting funds for vague purposes; many letters ask for loans for home repairs, for family illnesses; a Secaucus, New Jersey, student is $1,500 short on his tuition; and a young lady in New Mexico, with sexy photo enclosed, would like financing to prepare herself for the next Miss America contest.

There are many requests that move us, but we cannot give to individuals, only to certified organizations. Thus, we can only commiserate with the plight of a sixty-year-old widow who is losing her homestead of thirty years; a boy from Florida who needs school clothes; a mother whose son is dying of cancer and has a last request to visit Hawaii.

Some people are suspicious of altruism, and occasionally we

get cynical letters accusing Paul of giving all this money away so that he can gain a huge tax deduction. The fact is, however, that our corporate setup is such that, although we pay no taxes on the money we give away, Paul gets no other tax deductions from any of his regular income.

The rest is history. Although neither of us knew beans about business, we somehow managed to take all the right turns, and we enjoy the flood of truly gratifying letters we receive.

In the fall of 1984, one of these letters was received by the Newman's Own office, written by Sister Carol Putnam, a Sacred Heart nun who runs the Hope Rural School in Indiantown, Florida: "I am hurting desperately for help for a new bus. Ours does not pass inspection for the fall. A new bus costs $26,000. I have written to several sources and have gotten a 'No' so far. A bus will last us ten years, and we cannot pick up the children without one."

We phoned Sister Carol and discovered that Hope Rural, which is a school for the children of migrant farm workers, might have to go out of existence because its fourteen-year-old secondhand school bus had been condemned.

For years, the children had been denied any sort of consistent schooling. They were prevented from attending classes by the wretched poverty that forced their farm worker families to travel constantly throughout the country in search of seasonal work. The youngsters often labored in the fields alongside their parents, returning to central Florida every winter to harvest the state's citrus crops. When lucky, they lived in labor camps and abandoned houses; when times got particularly hard, they slept under bridges and in cars. Many of them had never held a schoolbook or heard a nursery rhyme until five years ago, when the Hope Rural School began a flexible term that allowed the children to attend classes during the picking season without having to enroll in a normal September-to-June school year.

"But when our school bus was condemned this past summer by the state authorities, my worst fears were realized," Sister Carol told us. "With no bus to transport these children from their homes miles away, the school would be worthless, and many of the children would return to their hopeless lives in the fields."

We sent a check that very day, for the immediate delivery of a new bus to Hope Rural, and as luck would have it, the new bus arrived a day after the license on the old bus expired.

To express their appreciation, the children of the Hope Rural School, which has classes from kindergarten through fourth grade, sent "Mr. Newman" the hand-drawn thank-you notes reprinted on these pages.

A. E. Hotchner

POSTSCRIPT

"What I like is when life wiggles its hips and throws me a surprise. All the experts said we couldn't produce these foods without chemical preservatives; they said we couldn't use fresh garlic and onions; they said we had to advertise; they said no business in the world could give away 100 percent of its profits. Well, we didn't listen to any of 'em, and just look at us. I feel that spreading our products around is spreading the gospel, and I'll stay at it as long as I enjoy it – and, as of now, I'm having a fine time."

P. Loquesto Newman

INDEX

Reprinted by permission: Tribune Media Services

The publishers hope that this book has given you enjoyable reading. Large Print Books are specially designed to be as easy to see and hold as possible. If you wish a complete list of our books, please ask at your local library or write directly to:
John Curley & Associates, Inc.
P.O. Box 37, South Yarmouth, Massachusetts, 02664.